THROUGH TIME INTO HEALING

ALSO BY DR BRIAN WEISS

Many Lives, Many Masters

Only Love is Real

Messages from the Masters

Meditation: Achieving Inner Peace and Tranquility in Your Life

THROUGH TIME INTO HEALING

How past life regression therapy can heal mind, body and soul

DR BRIAN WEISS

INTRODUCTION BY DR RAYMOND MOODY

The Twelve Steps are reprinted with permission of Alcoholics Anonymous World Services, Inc. Permission to reprint this material does not mean that AA has reviewed or approved the contents of this publication, nor that AA agrees with the views expressed herein. AA is a program of recovery from alcoholism– use of the Twelve Steps in connection with programs and activities which are patterned after AA, but which address other problems, does not imply otherwise.

First published in Great Britain in 1995
by Piatkus Books Ltd
5 Windmill Street, London W1T 2JA
email: info@piatkus.co.uk

This edition published in 1998

Reprinted 1998, 2001 (twice), 2003 (twice), 2005 (twice), 2006 (twice), 2007

A catalogue record for this book is available from the British Library

ISBN 978-0-7499-1835-4

Printed and bound in Great Britain by
Mackays of Chatham Ltd, Chatham, Kent

Acknowledgments

MY DEEP APPRECIATION GOES TO FRED HILLS, BARBARA Gess, and Bob Bender, all wonderful editors at Simon & Schuster, whose direction, encouragement, and expertise helped me so much with this book.

I also sincerely thank Deborah Bergman, my outside editor, who skillfully adjusted and improved the structure of my free-flowing first draft.

My heartfelt thanks go to Lois de la Haba, my literary agent, who has also become my friend.

And, finally, my deepest gratitude goes to all my patients, who are constantly teaching me about life and love.

To Carole, Jordan, and Amy,
My family,
I love you dearly and forever

Contents

THROUGH TIME INTO HEALING

Introduction

DURING THE PAST TWENTY YEARS OR SO, AND SO GRADually that we have hardly realized it, we in Western society have undergone a kind of revolution in consciousness. There is now a whole generation of young people who have grown up regularly hearing and reading of near death experiences, past life regressions, out of the body journeys, apparitions of the deceased, and a host of other remarkable phenomena of the spiritual life. I often have the pleasure and privilege of lecturing before college-age people, and I am still a bit startled to hear them speak so calmly and so naturally of their own visions and of their otherworldly travels.

When public interest in near death experiences began in 1975, some dismissed it as a fad. I am beginning to realize now, seventeen years later, that the near death experience is an established fact in our culture. I believe that we are on the verge of becoming (if we have not indeed already become) one of the many historical societies in which the visionary capacity of human beings is accepted as a matter of course. More and more, ordinary people are becoming comfortable talking about their visions and in exchanging information about various techniques for inducing or facilitating them.

Some fairly astonishing developments are coming out of research conducted by such investigators as Dr. Brian Weiss, Dr. William Roll, Dr. Ken Ring, Dr. Bruce Greyson, Dr. Melvin Morse, and a host of other physicians and psychologists in the United States, Europe, and elsewhere. I am fairly confident that within the next few years this research will proceed to the point at which profound experiences that can at least be called "psychic" and which may well be called "spiritual" can be readily facilitated in psychologically normal individuals. Just to give one example: during the past year, working with colleagues, I have developed a technique through which normal, psychologically stable adults, in a waking state of awareness, can experience vivid, full-color, three-dimensional, full-sized, moving apparitions of departed loved ones. Furthermore, much to my own surprise, my subjects—who so far have all been professionals of a decidedly sober temperament—have insisted on the "reality" of their encounters; they all believed that, in fact, they had seen and been in the presence of deceased relatives and friends. Indeed, I have now had such an experience myself—I sat with my grandmother who died some years ago and had a conversation that was every bit as real as any encounter I ever had with her while she was "alive." As a matter of fact, one of the most amazing things about this event, in which I joined the legions of everyday people all over the world who have experienced such happenings, was how absolutely normal and natural it seemed—indeed not in the very least spooky, not even unsettling.

What is happening, I believe, is that collectively we are opening up within ourselves and among ourselves to altered states of consciousness that were well understood among our ancestors in remote times but that were suppressed at a certain point in the development of our civilization, dismissed as superstitious or even as demonic. In my opinion, there is a chance that this development can be of great benefit to humankind. Václac Havel, the writer who is president of Czechoslovakia, gave a stirring speech to the Congress of the United States in which he stated firmly his belief that it is only through a worldwide revolution in human consciousness that we will be able to turn the world away from its present course toward annihilation. The former Russian President, Mr. Gorbachev, has himself seconded this opinion when he said that spiritual renewal is necessary to save his distraught country.

The past life regressions upon which Dr. Brian Weiss reports in this book are one example of the extraordinary phenomena of human consciousness that are now enjoying widespread acceptance. No one need feel in the least awkward or ashamed for having had such experiences. One of the great historians of our modern age, Sir Arnold Toynbee, relates how he was inspired to write his own monumental historical work by personal experiences that were—albeit spontaneous—obviously very similar to those which Brian Weiss describes.

People who return from near death experiences tell us that in the seeming closing moments of their earthly lives they learned that the most important thing we can do while here is learn to love. It now appears that this is the only way we can turn the world around, and we may well find that developing techniques that alter consciousness is the best way of accomplishing this end.

Brian Weiss is truly a pioneer in bringing to broader public awareness safe techniques for alteration of consciousness that may result in enhanced self-knowledge and that may promote better understanding among all people. Especially in this age of worldwide electronic media, it is possible that we may be able to bring about a spiritual renewal in which people all over the world are brought together in love and peace through the propagation of just such techniques as Dr. Weiss and others have developed.

Dr Raymond A. Moody

1

The Beginning

FOR THOSE OF YOU WHO HAVE NOT READ MY BOOK, *Many Lives, Many Masters*, a few words of introduction are necessary. You need to know something about me before we begin the work of healing.

Until my incredible experiences with Catherine, the patient whose therapy is described in the book, my professional life had been unidirectional and highly academic. I was graduated magna cum laude, Phi Beta Kappa, from Columbia University and received my medical degree from the Yale University School of Medicine, where I was also chief resident in psychiatry. I have been a professor at several prestigious university medical schools, and I have published over forty scientific papers in the fields of psychopharmacology, brain chemistry, sleep disorders, depression, anxiety states, substance abuse disorders, and Alzheimer's disease. My only previous contribution to book publishing had been *The Biology of Cholinergic Function*, which was hardly a best-seller, although reading it did help some of my insomniac patients fall asleep. I was left-brained, obsessive-compulsive, and completely skeptical of "unscientific" fields such as parapsychology. I knew nothing about the concept of past lives or reincarnation, nor did I want to.

Catherine was a patient who was referred to me about a year after I had become Chairman of the Department of Psychiatry at Mount Sinai Medical Center in Miami Beach, Florida. In her late twenties, a Catholic woman from New England, Catherine was quite comfortable with her religion, not questioning this part of her life. She was suffering from fears, phobias, paralyzing panic attacks, depression, and recurrent nightmares. Her symptoms had been lifelong and were now worsening.

After more than a year of conventional psychotherapy, she remained severely impaired. I felt she should have been more improved at the end of that time span. A hospital laboratory technician, she had the intelligence and insight to benefit from therapy. There was nothing in her basic makeup to suggest that her case would be a difficult one. Indeed, her background suggested a good prognosis. Since Catherine had a chronic fear of gagging and choking, she refused all medications, so I could not use antidepressants or tranquilizers, drugs I was trained to use to treat symptoms like hers. Her refusal turned out to be a blessing in disguise, although I did not realize it at that time.

Finally, Catherine consented to try hypnosis, a form of focused concentration, to remember back to her childhood and attempt to find the repressed or forgotten traumas that I felt must be causing her current symptoms.

Catherine was able to enter a deep hypnotic trance state, and she began to remember events that she consciously had been unable to recall. She remembered being pushed from a diving board and choking while in the water. She also recalled being frightened by the gas mask placed on her face in a dentist's office, and, worst of all, she remembered being fondled by her alcoholic father when she was three years old, his huge hand held over her mouth to keep her quiet. I was certain that now we had the answers. I was equally certain that now she would get better.

But her symptoms remained severe. I was very surprised. I had expected more of a response. As I pondered this stalemate, I concluded that there must be more traumas still buried in her subconscious. If her father had fondled her when she was three, perhaps he had done this at an even earlier age. We would try again.

The next week I once again hypnotized Catherine to a deep level. But this time, I inadvertently gave her an open-ended, non-directive instruction.

"Go back to the time from which your symptoms arise," I suggested.

I had expected Catherine to return once again to her early childhood.

Instead, she flipped back about four thousand years into an ancient near-Eastern lifetime, one in which she had a different face and body, different hair, a different name. She remembered details of topography, clothes, and everyday items from that time. She recalled events in that lifetime until ultimately she drowned in a flood or tidal wave, as her baby was torn from her arms by the force of the water. As Catherine died, she floated above her body, replicating the near death experience work of Dr. Elisabeth Kübler-Ross, Dr. Raymond Moody, Dr. Kenneth Ring, and others, work we will discuss in detail later in this book. Yet, she had never heard of these people or their work.

During this hypnosis session, Catherine remembered two other lifetimes. In one, she was a Spanish prostitute in the eighteenth century, and in another, a Greek woman who had lived a few hundred years after the near-Eastern lifetime.

I was shocked and skeptical. I had hypnotized hundreds of patients over the years, but this had never happened before. I had come to know Catherine well over the course of more than a year of intensive psychotherapy. I knew that she was not psychotic, did not hallucinate, did not have multiple personalities, was not particularly suggestible, and did not abuse drugs or alcohol. I concluded that her "memories" must have consisted of fantasy or dreamlike material.

But something very unusual happened. Catherine's symptoms began to improve dramatically, and I knew that fantasy or dreamlike material would not lead to such a fast and complete clinical cure. Week by week, this patient's formerly intractable symptoms disappeared as under hypnosis she remembered more past lives. Within a few months she was totally cured, without the use of any medicines.

My considerable skepticism was gradually eroding. During the fourth or fifth hypnosis session something even stranger transpired. After reliving a death in an ancient lifetime, Catherine floated above her body and was drawn to the familiar spiritual light she always encountered in the in-between-lifetimes state.

"They tell me there are many gods, for God is in each of us," she told me in a husky voice. And then she completely changed the rest of my life:

> "Your father is here, and your son, who is a small child. Your father says you will know him because his name is Avrom, and your daughter is named after him. Also, his death was due to his heart. Your son's heart was also important, for it was backward, like a chicken's. He made a great sacrifice for you out of his love. His soul is very advanced . . . his death satisfied his parents' debts. Also he wanted to show you that medicine could only go so far, that its scope is very limited."

Catherine stopped speaking, and I sat in an awed silence as my numbed mind tried to sort things out. The room felt icy cold.

Catherine knew very little about my personal life. On my desk I had a baby picture of my daughter, grinning happily with her two bottom baby teeth in an otherwise empty mouth. My son's picture was next to it. Otherwise Catherine knew virtually nothing about my family or my personal history. I had been well schooled in traditional psychotherapeutic techniques. The therapist was supposed to be a tabula rasa, a blank tablet upon which the patient could project her own feelings, thoughts, and attitudes. These then could be analyzed by the therapist, enlarging the arena of the patient's mind. I had kept this therapeutic distance with Catherine. She knew me only as a psychiatrist, knew nothing of my past or of my private life. I had never even displayed my diplomas in the office.

The greatest tragedy in my life had been the unexpected death of our firstborn son, Adam, who was only twenty-three days old when he died early in 1971. About ten days after we had brought him home from the hospital, he had developed respiratory problems and projectile vomiting. The diagnosis was extremely difficult to make. "Total anomalous pulmonary venous drainage with an atrial septal defect," we were told. "It occurs once in approximately every ten million births." The pulmonary veins, which were supposed to bring oxygenated blood back to the heart, were incorrectly routed, entering the heart on the wrong side. It was as if his heart were turned around, *backward*. Extremely, extremely rare.

Heroic open-heart surgery could not save Adam, who died several days later. We mourned for months, our hopes and dreams dashed. Our son, Jordan, was born a year later, a grateful balm for our wounds.

At the time of Adam's death, I had been wavering about my earlier choice of psychiatry as a career. I was enjoying my internship in internal medicine, and I had been offered a residency position in medicine. After Adam's death, I firmly decided that I would make psychiatry my profession. I was angry that modern medicine, with all of its advanced skills and technology, could not save my son, this simple, tiny baby.

My father had been in excellent health until he experienced a massive heart attack early in 1979, at the age of sixty-one. He survived the initial attack, but his heart wall had been irretrievably damaged, and he died three days later. This was about nine months before Catherine's first appointment.

My father had been a religious man, more ritualistic than spiritual. His Hebrew name, Avrom, suited him better than the English, Alvin. Four months after his death, our daughter, Amy, was born, and she was named after him.

Here in 1982 in my quiet, darkened office, a deafening cascade of hidden, secret truths was pouring upon me. I was swimming in a spiritual sea, and I loved the water. My arms were gooseflesh. Catherine could not possibly know this information. There was no place even to look it up. My father's *Hebrew* name, that I had a son who died in infancy from a one-in-ten million heart defect, my brooding about medicine, my father's death, and my daughter's naming—it was too much, too specific, too true. This unsophisticated laboratory technician was a conduit for transcendental knowledge. And if she could reveal these truths, what else was there? I needed to know more.

"Who," I sputtered, "who is there? Who tells you these things?"

"The Masters," she whispered, "the Master Spirits tell me. They tell me I have lived eighty-six times in physical state."[1]

[1] *Many Lives, Many Masters*, pp. 54–56.

I knew that Catherine did not and could not know these facts. My father died in New Jersey, and he was buried in upstate New York. He did not even have an obituary. Adam had died a decade earlier in New York City, twelve hundred miles away. Very few of my close friends in Florida knew about Adam. Even fewer knew the circumstances of his death. Certainly no one at the hospital did. Catherine had no way of knowing any of this family history. Yet she had said "Avrom," and not the English translation, Alvin.

After the shock subsided, I returned to the behavior of an obsessive-compulsive, scientifically trained psychiatrist. I scoured the libraries and bookstores for more information. I found some excellent work, such as Dr. Ian Stevenson's research with young children who have demonstrated reincarnational-type memories, research that we will briefly discuss later in this book. I also found a few published studies of clinicians who had used past life regression, which is the use of hypnosis and other related techniques that allow the patient's subconscious mind to go back in time to retrieve memories from prior lifetimes. I now know that many more clinicians are afraid to go public, fearing the reactions, worrying about their careers and reputations.

Catherine, whose story is described in complete detail in *Many Lives, Many Masters*, traversed a dozen of her lifetimes, and she was cured. She continues to lead a happier, more joyful life, freed from her paralyzing symptoms and from her pervasive fear of death. She knows that a part of her containing her memory and personality and yet possessing a far greater perspective than her conscious mind will survive her physical death.

After my experience with Catherine, my perspective on psychotherapy began to change radically. I realized that past life therapy offered a rapid method of treating psychiatric symptoms, symptoms that had previously taken many months or years of costly therapy to alleviate. Here was a much more direct way to heal pain and fear. I began to use this therapy on other patients and again had excellent results. At the time of this writing, I have regressed hundreds of patients to past lives during their individual therapy sessions. I have regressed many times that number in group workshops.

Who are my patients? They are physicians, attorneys, business executives, other therapists, housewives, blue-collar workers, salespersons, and so on. They are people from different religions, socioeconomic levels, educational backgrounds, and belief systems. Yet, many of them have been able to remember details from other lifetimes, and many of them have been able to remember survival after physical death.

Most of my patients experienced past life regressions through hypnosis. However, others remembered previous lives through meditation, or spontaneously while experiencing intense déjà vu feelings, or through vivid dreams, or in other ways.

Many were able to rid themselves of chronic lifelong symptoms, such as specific phobias, panic attacks, recurrent nightmares, unexplained fears, obesity, repeated destructive relationships, physical pain and illness, and so on.

This is not a placebo effect. Generally, these are not people who are gullible or suggestible. They remember—names, dates, geography, details. And after they remember, like Catherine, they become cured.

Perhaps even more important than the curing of specific physical and emotional symptoms is the knowledge that we do not die when our bodies do. We are immortal. We do survive physical death.

Through Time into Healing chronicles what I have learned about the healing potential of past life regression since *Many Lives, Many Masters* was completed. The case stories are all true. Only the names and identifying information have been altered.

2

Hypnosis and Regression

HYPNOSIS IS THE MAIN TECHNIQUE I USE TO HELP PAtients access past life memories. Many people have questions about what hypnosis is and about what happens when a person is in a hypnotic state, but there is really no mystery. Hypnosis is a state of focused concentration, of the sort many of us experience every day.

When you are relaxed and your concentration is so intense that you are not distracted by outside noises or other stimuli, you are in a light state of hypnosis. All hypnosis is really self-hypnosis in that you, the patient, control the process. The therapist is merely a guide. Most of us enter hypnotic states every day—when we are absorbed in a good book or movie, when we have driven our car the last few blocks home without realizing how we got there, whenever we have been on "automatic pilot."

One goal of hypnosis, as well as meditation, is to access the subconscious. This is the part of our mind that lies beneath ordinary consciousness, beneath the constant bombardment of thoughts, feelings, outside stimuli, and other assaults on our awareness. The subconscious mind functions at a level deeper than our usual level of awareness. In the subconscious mind mental processes occur without our conscious perception of them. We experience moments of intuition, wisdom, and creativity when these subconscious processes flash into our conscious awareness.

The subconscious is not limited by our imposed boundaries of logic, space, and time. It can remember everything, from any time. It can transmit creative solutions to our problems. It can transcend the ordinary to touch upon a wisdom far beyond our everyday capabilities. Hypnosis accesses the wisdom of the subconscious in a focused way in order to achieve healing. We are in hypnosis whenever the usual relationship between the conscious and subconscious mind is reconfigured so that the subconscious plays a more dominant role. There is a broad spectrum of hypnotic techniques. They are designed to tap into a broad spectrum of hypnotic states, from light to deep levels.

In a way, hypnosis is a continuum in which we are aware of the conscious and subconscious mind to a greater or lesser degree. I have found that many people can be hypnotized to a degree suitable for therapy if they are educated about hypnosis and if their fears are discussed and allayed. The majority of the public has misconceptions about hypnosis because of the way television, movies, and stage shows have depicted it.

When you are hypnotized, you are *not* asleep. Your conscious mind is always aware of what you are experiencing while you are hypnotized. Despite the deep subconscious contact, your mind can comment, criticize, and censor. You are always in control of what you say. Hypnosis is *not* a "truth serum." You do not enter a time machine and suddenly find yourself transported to another time and place with no awareness of the present. Some people in hypnosis watch the past as if they are observing a movie. Others are more vividly involved, with more emotional reactions. Still others "feel" things more than they "see" them. Sometimes the predominant reaction is that of hearing or even smelling. Afterwards, the person remembers everything experienced during the hypnosis session.

It may sound as though it requires a great deal of skill to reach these deeper levels of hypnosis. However, each of us experiences them with ease every day as we pass through the state between wakefulness and sleeping known as the hypnagogic state. We are in a type of hypnagogic state when we are just waking up and can still remember our dreams vividly, but we are not yet fully awake. It is the period before everyday memories and concerns reenter our minds. Like hypnosis, the hypnagogic state is a deeply creative one. When we pass through it, the mind is completely turned inward and can access the inspiration of the subconscious. The hypnagogic state is considered by many to be a "genius" state, without any boundaries or any limitations. When we are hypnagogic, we have access to all our resources and none of our self-imposed restrictions.

Thomas Edison valued this hypnagogic state so highly that he developed his own technique to maintain it while he worked on his inventions. While sitting in a certain chair, Edison used relaxation and meditation techniques to reach the state of consciousness that is between sleep and wakefulness. He would hold some ball bearings in his closed hand, palm down, while resting this hand on the arm of his chair. Beneath his hand he kept a metal bowl. If Edison fell asleep, his hand would open. The ball bearings would fall into the metal bowl and the noise would awaken him. Then he would repeat the process over and over again.

This hypnagogic state is very much like hypnosis and actually deeper than many levels of hypnosis. By helping the patient to reach a deeper level of his or her mind, a therapist who is skilled in the techniques of hypnosis can dramatically accelerate the healing process. And when creative ideas and solutions extend beyond personal problems, large segments of society can benefit, as all of us have benefited from Thomas Edison's invention of the light bulb. The process can touch the world.

Listening to someone's guiding voice aids in focusing concentration and helps a patient to reach a deeper level of hypnosis and relaxation. There is no danger in hypnosis. Not one person I have ever hypnotized has become "stuck" in the hypnotic state. You can emerge from a state of hypnosis whenever you want. No one has ever violated his or her moral and ethical principles. No one has involuntarily acted like a chicken or a duck. No one can control you. You are in complete control.

In hypnosis, your mind is always aware and observing. This is why people who may be deeply hypnotized and actively involved in a childhood or past life sequence of memories are able to answer the therapist's questions, speak their current life language, know the geographical places they are seeing, and even know the year, which usually flashes before their inner eyes or just appears in their minds. The hypnotized mind, always retaining an awareness and a knowledge of the present, puts the childhood or past life memories into context. If the year 1900 flashes, and you find yourself building a pyramid in ancient Egypt, you *know* that the year is B.C., even if you don't see those actual letters.

This is also the reason why a hypnotized patient, finding himself a peasant fighting in a medieval European war, for example, can recognize people from that past lifetime whom he knows in his current life. This is why he can speak modern English, compare the crude weapons of that time with those he might have seen or used in this lifetime, give dates, and so on.

His present-day mind is aware, watching, commenting. He can always compare the details and events with those of his current life. He is the movie's observer and its critic and usually its star at the same time. And all the while, he can remain in the relaxed, hypnotized state.

Hypnosis puts the patient in a state that holds great potential for healing by giving the patient access to the subconscious mind. To speak metaphorically, it puts the patient in the magical forest that holds the healing tree. But if hypnosis lets the patient into that healing country, it is the regression process that is the tree that holds the sacred berries he or she must eat to heal.

Regression therapy is the mental act of going back to an earlier time, whenever that time may be, in order to retrieve memories that may still be negatively influencing a patient's present life and that are probably the source of the patient's symptoms. Hypnosis allows the mind to short-circuit conscious barriers to tap this information, including those barriers that prevent patients from consciously accessing their past lives.

Repetition compulsion is the name given by Freud to describe the often irresistible urge to redramatize or reenact emotional, typically painful, experiences that occurred in one's past. In his

Papers on Psycho-Analysis (1938), the famous British psychoanalyst Ernest Jones defines repetition compulsion as "the blind impulse to repeat earlier experiences and situations quite irrespective of any advantage that doing so might bring from a pleasure-pain point of view." No matter how harmful and destructive the behavior, the person seems compelled to repeat it. Willpower is ineffective in controlling the compulsion.

Freud discovered that bringing the initial trauma to consciousness, cathartically releasing it (a process therapists call abreaction), and integrating what has been felt and learned is effective. Hypnotic regression therapy performed by a skilled therapist first puts the patient in a hypnotic state and then gives the patient the tools needed to bring an incident like this to light. Often, the incident occurred during childhood. This is standard psychoanalytic theory.

But other times, as I discovered while treating Catherine, the initial trauma stretches backward much farther than that, into past lives. I have found that about 40 percent of my patients need to delve into other lifetimes to resolve their current life clinical problems. Regression to an earlier period of this present-day lifetime is usually fruitful enough for most of the remainder.

For those first 40 percent, however, regression to previous lifetimes is key to a cure. The best therapist working within the classically accepted limits of the single lifetime will not be able to effect a complete cure for the patient whose symptoms were caused by a trauma that occurred in a previous lifetime, perhaps hundreds or even thousands of years ago. But when past life therapy is used to bring these long-repressed memories to awareness, improvement in the current symptoms is usually swift and dramatic.

A pattern of compulsive sexual acting out would be one example of a repetition compulsion syndrome. I know of a young man who is compulsively driven by a form of exhibitionism, specifically of exposing his genitalia to certain women while masturbating in a car. This behavior is obviously dangerous and destructive. This young man has outraged women, and he has been arrested several times. Yet, his destructive compulsion continues to occur.

His therapist has traced the origins of this behavior back to sexual incidents that occurred between this young man and his mother when he was quite young. This mother used to fondle her son while she bathed him, and he would consequently have erections. Confusing, arousing, and disturbing feelings were elicited in this child. These feelings were extremely intense, and part of the young man's compulsion seemed to be a desire to recreate the intensity of these earlier emotions.

Despite this excellent therapist's success in uncovering an early trauma, this man's therapy has been successful only in part, and he suffers frequent relapses. Even though his behavior causes him to feel profound guilt and shame in addition to subjecting him to other dangers, he experiences overwhelming urges to repeat it.

Based on my experience with over three hundred individual past life regression patients, there is a good possibility that the reason this therapy has been only partially successful lies in the fact that the *original* trauma may have occurred in a prior lifetime. The scenario may even have been repeated in several lifetimes. Perhaps the most recent manifestation, the one experienced in his current life, is only the latest in a series of similar traumas. The recurrent pattern has already been established. All of the traumas, not just the most recent, need to be brought to awareness. Then complete healing can occur.

Many of my patients have recalled different traumatic patterns under hypnosis that repeat in various forms in lifetime after lifetime. These patterns include abuse between father and daughter that has been recurring over centuries only to surface once again in the current life. They also include an abusive husband in a past life who has resurfaced in the present as a violent father. Alcoholism is a condition that has ruined several lifetimes, and one warring couple discovered they had been homicidally connected in four previous lives together.

Many of these patients had been in conventional therapy before they came to see me, but their therapy had been ineffective or only partially effective. For these patients, regression therapy to past lifetimes was necessary to completely eradicate symptoms and to permanently end these recurring cycles of harmful, maladaptive behavior.

The concept of repetition compulsion seems valid. However, the scope of the past must be enlarged to include past lives if uncovering the present lifetime's sources proves unsuccessful. I am certain that the young man who is compelled to masturbate while driving needs to explore his past life realms, to identify the traumas, and to bring them into his current awareness. When the pathological foundation is still covertly present, the symptoms will inevitably recur. Only when it is brought to light can he really be cured.

I have found that hypnosis combined with regression therapy plumbs the unconscious more deeply than do psychoanalytic techniques like free association, in which the patient remains in a relaxed but conscious state while merely closing the eyes. Because it promotes a deeper strata of associations by tapping memory storage areas unavailable to the conscious mind, hypnotic regression therapy offers many patients deeper and dramatically rapid results.

The material tapped by past life therapy is in some ways like the powerful universal archetypes described by Carl Jung. However, the material of past life regression therapy is not archetypal or symbolic but actual memory fragments of the ongoing current of human experience from ancient times to the present. Past life regression therapy combines the specificity and healing catharsis that is the best of Freudian therapy with the healing participation and recognition of deep symbolic meaning that is the hallmark of Jung.

But regression therapy consists of much more than hypnotic technique. Before the hypnotic process can be initiated, a skilled regression therapist will spend a great deal of time taking a history, asking questions, getting answers, and going very specifically and in great detail into particular areas of importance. This increases the success rate of regression from about 50 percent to about 70 percent. And after the regression is completed, after the patient has emerged from the hypnotic state, it is then necessary to integrate the feelings, insights, and information the session has elicited into the current life situation.

This integration requires considerable therapeutic skill and experience because the material evoked is often powerful and emotionally charged. Therefore, I do not recommend past life therapy done by a therapist who is not certified or accredited by a traditional accrediting body, who does not have a degree such as M.D., Ph.D., M.S.W., or other traditional degrees. Nontraditional past life therapists may be less likely to let a memory evolve at its own pace and less likely to have the skills necessary to help the patient integrate the material.

Experiencing a past life regression alone at home, however, is beneficial and relaxing in most cases. The subconscious is wise and will not provide the conscious mind with a memory it is not capable of assimilating. There is a slight risk of adverse symptoms such as anxiety or guilt, but these can be alleviated, if necessary, by a visit to a trained therapist. An individual who has even a slightly adverse reaction while working alone will simply stop the experience, his subconscious protecting him, while an untrained therapist might try to override the subconscious and push that individual to continue before the client is ready.

As a psychiatrist with a hectic clinical schedule, my main priority is to cure my patients rather than to validate their past life memories—although such validation is also extremely important.

I find that actual past life memories are accessed and described by the patient in one of two patterns. I call the first pattern the *classical* pattern. In the classical pattern, a patient enters a lifetime and is able to offer a very complete level of detail about the life and its events. Almost like a story, much of the entire lifetime passes by, often beginning with birth or childhood and not ending until death. It is possible that the patient will painlessly and serenely experience the death scene and a life review, in which the lessons of the lifetime are illuminated and discussed with the benefit of the patient's higher wisdom and possibly by religious figures or spiritual guides.

Many of Catherine's lifetimes were recalled in the classical regression pattern. Here is an excerpt of one of them, a lifetime, apparently Egyptian, in which Catherine began by recalling a water-borne plague that had killed her father and brother. She had worked with the priests who prepared the bodies for burial.

At the time the memory began and also in this excerpt of it Catherine was sixteen:

"People were put in caves. The bodies were kept in caves. But first, the bodies had to be prepared by the priests. They must be wrapped and anointed. They were kept in caves, but the land is flooding . . . They say the water is bad. Don't drink the water."

"Is there a way of treating it? Did anything work?"

"We were given herbs, different herbs. The odors . . . the herbs and . . . smell the odor. I can smell it!"

"Do you recognize the smell?"

"It's white. They hang it from the ceiling."

"Is it like garlic?"

"It's hung around . . . the properties are similar, yes. . . . You put it in your mouth, your ears, your nose, everywhere. The odor was strong. It was believed to block the evil spirits from entering your body. Purple . . . fruit or something round with purple covering, purple skin to it . . ."

. . . "Is the purple a fruit of some sort?"

"Tannis."

"Would that help you? Is that for the illness?"

"It was at that time."

"Tannis," I repeated again, trying to see if she was talking about what we refer to as tannin or tannic acid. . . . "What in this lifetime has buried itself in your current lifetime? Why do you keep coming back here? What is it that is so uncomfortable?"

"The religion," Catherine quickly whispered, "the religion of that time. It was a religion of fear . . . fear. There were so many things to fear . . . and so many gods."

"Do you remember the names of any gods?"

"I see eyes. I see a black . . . some type of . . . it looks like a jackal. He's in a statue. He's a guardian of some type . . . I see a woman, a goddess, with some type of headpiece on."

"Do you know her name, the goddess?"

"Osiris . . . Sirus . . . something like that. I see an eye . . . eye, just an eye, an eye on a chain. It's gold."

"An eye?"

"Yes. . . . Hathor! Who is that!"

I had never heard of Hathor, although I knew that Osiris, if the pronunciation was accurate, was the brother-husband of Isis, a major

Egyptian deity. Hathor, I later learned, was the Egyptian goddess of love, mirth, and joy. "Is it one of the gods?" I asked.

"Hathor! Hathor." There was a long pause. "Bird . . . he's flat . . . flat, a phoenix." She was silent again.

"Go ahead in time now to your final day in that lifetime. Go to your final day, but before you have died. Tell me what you see."

She answered in a very soft whisper. "I see people and buildings. I see sandals, sandals. There is a rough cloth, some type of rough cloth."

"What happens? Go to the time of your dying now. What happens to you? You can see it."

"I do not see it . . . I don't see *me* any more."

"Where are you? What do you see?"

"Nothing . . . just darkness. . . . I see a light, a warm light." She had already died, already passed over to the spiritual state. Apparently she did not need to experience her actual death again.

"Can you come to the light?" I asked.

"I am going." She was resting peacefully, waiting again.

"Can you look backward now to the lessons of that lifetime? Are you aware of them yet?"

"No," she whispered. She continued to wait. Suddenly she appeared alert, although her eyes remained closed. . . . Her voice was louder. "I feel . . . someone's talking to me!"

"What do they say?"

"Talking about patience. One must have patience . . ."

"Yes, go on."

The answer came from the poet Master. "Patience and timing . . . everything comes when it must come. A life cannot be rushed, cannot be worked on a schedule as so many people want it to be. We must accept what comes to us at a given time, and not ask for more. But life is endless, so we never die; we were never really born. We just pass through different phases. There is no end. Humans have many dimensions. But time is not as we see time, but rather in lessons that are learned."[1]

The details of burial, the herb that was used to ward off sickness, and the statues of gods are all typical of classical regression.

[1] *Many Lives, Many Masters*, pp. 108–112.

So is the wide span of time that the memory covers, from sixteen until death. Although Catherine did not remember the actual death experience here (she had recalled the death experience from this lifetime in a previous session), she did pass through it to receive illuminating spiritual information on the "other side."

The second pattern of past life recall is one I call the ***key moment flow*** pattern. In key moment flow, the subconscious knits together the most important or relevant moments from a cluster of lifetimes, the key moments that will best elucidate the hidden trauma and most quickly and powerfully heal the patient.

Sometimes the flow includes the between-life review, and sometimes it does not. Sometimes the lesson or pattern is subtle and does not become clear until close to the end of the flow or when I specifically ask the patient what it is. Other times the pattern is telegraphed instantly by the pattern and flow of key moment memory.

With some patients, key moment flow has a fragmentary quality that can expand either into a more detailed key moment flow or a classical pattern in later sessions, according to the optimal flow of memory and healing for the particular patient as determined by that patient's subconscious. Frequently, key moment flow moves dramatically and yet gently and peacefully from trauma to trauma, from death scene to death scene, as it weaves its own unblinking yet deeply healing form of illumination. Here are some examples of key moment flow, again from Catherine's case. These memories all come from Catherine's first past life regression session:

> "There are trees and a stone road. I see a fire with cooking. My hair is blond. I'm wearing a long, coarse brown dress and sandals. I am twenty-five. I have a girl child whose name is Cleastra . . . She's Rachel. [Rachel is presently her niece; they have always had an extremely close relationship.] It's very hot. . . . There are big waves knocking down trees. There's no place to run. It's cold; the water is cold. I have to save my baby, but I cannot . . . just have to hold her tight. I drown; the water chokes me. I can't breathe, can't swallow . . . salty water. My baby is torn out of my arms. . . . I see clouds

. . . My baby is with me. And others from my village. I see my brother."

She was resting; this lifetime had ended. She was still in a deep trance. . . .

"Go on," I said. . . . "Do you remember anything else?"

. . . "I have on a dress with black lace, and there is black lace on my head. I have dark hair with gray in it. It's [A.D.] 1756. I am Spanish. My name is Louisa and I'm fifty-six. I'm dancing; others are dancing, too. [Long pause]. I'm sick; I have a fever, cold sweats . . . Lots of people are sick; people are dying . . . The doctors don't know it was from the water." I took her ahead in time. "I recover, but my head still hurts, my eyes and head still hurt from the fever, from the water. Many die."[2]

Clearly, in this key moment flow the pattern is trauma experienced through natural disaster. The emotionally concentrated nature of key moment flow pattern may seem intense, but, in my experience, reliving the trauma or death scene runs only a minimal risk of incurring a disturbing reaction within either regression pattern. In the hands of a trained therapist and even working at home alone, most people handle and integrate the memories without difficulty. They actually feel much better. The therapist can always instruct them to float above the death scene, if they feel it is necessary, to observe without emotion, and the subconscious mind can always remove a patient from the regression experience. People can choose not to experience the death scene at all. There are always choices. But the intensity of past life therapy does not frighten those who experience it.

Past life therapy that flows from key moment to key moment is a very practical, successful therapy modality, one in which the necessary connections between past lives and present life may take place in perhaps less than one hour rather than in several hours. However, key moment flow tends to provide less validation for the patient than does the classical pattern, because its focus is on essence, not details.

I myself cannot predict which of these patterns a patient will adopt. Both heal equally.

[2] *Many Lives, Many Masters*, pp. 28–30.

Finally, not everyone needs to remember prior lifetimes through regression under hypnosis. Not every individual bears the weight of past life traumas or scars that are significant in the current lifetime. Often, what a patient needs is to concentrate on the present, not the past. However, I teach most of my patients self-hypnotic and meditative techniques, since these skills are enormously valuable in day-to-day life. Whether a patient wishes to cure insomnia, reduce high blood pressure, lose weight, stop smoking, augment the immune system to fight off infections and chronic diseases, reduce stress, or achieve states of relaxation and inner peace, these techniques can be effectively used for the rest of his or her life.

Despite the benefits, there are times when patients will nevertheless decline hypnosis. Often the reasons are surprising.

When I was a resident in psychiatry at Yale Medical School, a businessman was referred to me for treatment of his fear of flying. At that time, I was one of the few therapists at Yale who used hypnosis to cure monosymptomatic phobias, which are fears of one specific thing, such as flying, or driving on highways, or snakes. This businessman's job required a considerable amount of travelling. Since he would only use ground transportation, he clearly needed to overcome his fear.

I carefully outlined the hypnotic procedure. I transmitted my confidence and optimism that he could be cured, that he would no longer be paralyzed by his fear. Not only would this cure greatly help his business prospects, I assured him, but he would be able to vacation at more distant and exotic places. His whole life-style and quality of living would improve.

He looked pensively at me, frowning. Moments slowly passed. Why wasn't he more excited?

"No thanks, Doc," he finally said. "I'll pass on the treatment!"

This caught me completely off guard. I had successfully treated many patients with similar symptoms, and none had rejected my help.

"Why?" I asked. "Why don't you want to be cured?"

"Because I believe you, Doc. You *will* cure me. I won't be

afraid to fly. Then I'll get on the plane, and it'll take off, then crash, and I'll be dead. No thanks!"

I had no argument to counter his. He cordially left the office with his phobia intact, but he was undeniably still alive.

I was learning more about the human mind, its resistances and denials.

3

Through Experience into Understanding

OFTEN A NEW PATIENT OR WORKSHOP ATTENDEE CONfides to me, "Dr. Weiss, I'm very interested in experiencing past life regression, but I'm having some trouble accepting the concept of reincarnation."

If you feel like this, you are not alone. Many of these people need to address this issue before beginning the regression process. Doing this is often a preliminary part of therapy with these patients, and it is a common topic for questions and answers in my workshops and lectures. Before my extraordinary experiences with Catherine, I myself was extremely skeptical about the concept of reincarnation and the healing potential of past life regression. Even afterwards, it took several more years for me to make the commitment to bring my new beliefs and experiences into the public eye.

Although Catherine's therapy had radically changed my understanding of the nature of life and the nature of healing, I was hesitant to let other people know about these profound experiences because I was afraid I would be considered "crazy" or "weird" by colleagues and friends.

On the other hand, I had received further confirmation of the effectiveness of past life therapy by successfully treating more patients with this technique. I knew that I had to alleviate my discomfort, to resolve this issue. So I went to the medical library to see if other research was available. The left-brained, logical clinician in me liked this solution to the problem, and I hoped that such validation existed. If I had accidentally stumbled onto past life recall, I was certain that other psychiatrists using hypnotic techniques must have had similar experiences. Perhaps one of them had been brave enough to tell the tale.

I was disappointed to find only a few, albeit excellent, research reports. For instance, I found Dr. Ian Stevenson's documentation of cases in which children appeared to remember details of previous lives. Many of these details were later corroborated by investigative research. This was very important because it helped to provide validating proof of the concept of reincarnation. But there was little else to be found, certainly next to nothing about the therapeutic value of past life regression.

I left the library even more frustrated than when I had entered. How could this be possible? My own experience had already allowed me to hypothesize that past life recall could be a useful therapeutic tool for a variety of psychological and physical symptoms.

Why had no one else reported his or her experience? In addition, why was there almost no acknowledgment in the professional literature of past life experiences surfacing during clinical hypnotherapy? It seemed unlikely that these experiences were mine alone. Surely other therapists had had them.

In retrospect, I can see that what I really wanted was someone to have done the work that I would soon do. At that time I could only wonder whether other psychotherapists were as hesitant as I was to come forward. My research of the literature complete, I was torn between the power and reality of my own direct experiences and the fear that my ideas and new beliefs about life after death and contact with master guides might not be personally and professionally "appropriate."

I decided to consult another discipline. From my college religion course at Columbia University, I recalled how the major traditions of the East, Hinduism and Buddhism, embraced reincarnation as a central tenet, and how in these religions the concept of past lives is accepted as a basic aspect of reality. I had also learned that the Sufi tradition of Islam has a very beautiful tradition of reincarnation, rendered in poetry, dance, and song.

I simply could not believe that during the thousands of years of the history of Western religions no one had written about experiences like mine. I could not have been the first one to receive this information. I later discovered that in both Judaism and in Christianity the roots of belief in reincarnation go very deep.

In Judaism, a fundamental belief in reincarnation, or *gilgul*, has existed for thousands of years. This belief had been a basic cornerstone of the Jewish faith until approximately 1800–1850, when the urge to "modernize" and to be accepted by the more scientific Western establishment transformed the Eastern European Jewish communities. However, the belief in reincarnation had been fundamental and mainstream until this time, less than two centuries ago. In the Orthodox and Chasidic communities, belief in reincarnation continues unabated today. The Kabbala, mystical Jewish literature dating back thousands of years, is filled with references to reincarnation. Rabbi Moshe Chaim Luzzatto, one of the most brilliant Jewish scholars of the past several centuries, summed up *gilgul* in his book, *The Way of God:* "A single soul can be reincarnated a number of times in different bodies, and in this manner, it can rectify the damage done in previous incarnations. Similarly, it can also attain perfection that was not attained in its previous incarnations."

When I researched the history of Christianity, I discovered that early references to reincarnation in the New Testament had been deleted in the fourth century by Emperor Constantine when Christianity became the official religion of the Roman Empire. Apparently, the emperor had felt that the concept of reincarnation was threatening to the stability of the empire. Citizens who believed that they would have another chance to live might be less obedient and law abiding than those who believed in a single Judgment Day for all.

In the sixth century, the Second Council of Constantinople underscored Constantine's act by officially declaring reincarnation a heresy. Like Constantine, the Church was afraid that the idea of prior lives would weaken and undermine its growing power by affording followers too much time to seek salvation. They concurred that the whip of Judgment Day was necessary to ensure the proper attitudes and behavior.

During the same Early Christian Era leading up to the Council of Constantinople, other Church fathers like Origen, Clement of Alexandria, and St. Jerome accepted and believed in reincarnation. So did the Gnostics. As late as the twelfth century, the Christian Cathars of Italy and southern France were severely brutalized for their belief in reincarnation.

As I reflected on the new information I had gathered, I realized that aside from their belief in reincarnation, the Cathars, Gnostics, and Kabbalists all had another value in common: that direct personal experience beyond what we see and know with our rational minds or what is taught by a religious structure is a major source of spiritual wisdom. And this direct personal experience powerfully promotes spiritual and personal growth. Unfortunately, since people may be severely punished for unorthodox beliefs, the groups learned to keep them secret. The repression of past life teachings has been political, not spiritual.[1]

And so I began to understand the "whys." I myself was concerned that I might be punished for my beliefs if I made them public. Yet I know that people have the right to have access to the tools of growth and healing, and I have seen from my own clinical experience that past life regression can heal and transform people's lives. I also know that patients become *better*, more useful members of society and their families, with much more to offer.

But even after *Many Lives, Many Masters* was published, I was still waiting for the backlash. I was waiting for doctors to ridicule me, for my reputation to be tarnished and, perhaps, even for my family to suffer. My fears were unfounded. Although I hear there's a stray colleague or two who has been known to mutter

[1] See *Reincarnation: The Phoenix Fire Mystery* by Cranston and Head for an excellent study on the history of the political and social treatment of the concept of reincarnation in the West.

about "poor Brian who's only got one foot on the curb," instead of losing friends and colleagues, I gained more. I also began to receive letters—wonderful letters—from psychiatrists and psychologists throughout the country who had experiences like mine but had not dared to make them public.

This was a powerful lesson for me. I had taken the risk of documenting and presenting my experiences to the public and professional world, and my reward was knowledge, validation, and acceptance. In addition, I had learned that understanding does not always begin with reading accounts of studies in libraries. It can also come from exploring one's own experience. Intuition can lead one to intellect. The twain can meet; they can nourish and inspire each other. They had done so for me.

I tell this story because your concerns—the tug of war between your experiential and intellectual knowledge—might, in essence, be similar to mine. *Many* people have the same experiences and beliefs you do, perhaps many more than you can imagine. And many of these people feel discouraged from communicating their experiences for the same reasons you do. Still others may be expressing them, but in private. It is important to keep an open mind, to trust your experiences. Don't let the dogma and beliefs of others undermine your personal experience and perception of reality.

Another concern people have about past lives is whether it is "weird" to believe in psychic phenomena. This concern is easier to allay. Such experiences are universal. Discreetly poll some of your friends and family members about whether or not they have ever had any kind of precognitive dream or other psychic experience. You may find the results surprising.

I certainly did. Two months after *Many Lives, Many Masters* was published, I gave an informal talk to a book club composed of ten women who lived in Miami Beach. The group had been meeting for twelve years to discuss a wide range of books, mostly popular literature. They were not particularly interested in metaphysics. However, since I was a local author and willing to talk with them, the club read its first metaphysical book in its twelve years of existence. On the evening I attended, the discussion group consisted of all ten women. They were mostly middle class and mainstream and seemed to constitute a good cross section of that population.

Early in the discussion, I polled each member of the group about what her beliefs about reincarnation and life after death had been before reading *Many Lives, Many Masters*. Three women (30 percent) had believed in reincarnation. Six (60 percent), including the first three, believed in life after death, and four (40 percent) believed that they died when their bodies died. These statistics were very close to the national averages reported in a Gallup poll.

When I asked the club members whether they had ever personally experienced any psychic phenomena, I was surprised at the range and intensity of the responses I received. Remember, this was not a preselected, metaphysically oriented group with an ongoing interest in ESP, psychic events, or reincarnation. This was just a group of ten women who liked to read and discuss many different kinds of books.

One group member's mother had once been visited in a dream by her grandmother, who was elderly but not ill. In the dream, the grandmother was radiant and glowing, enveloped in a golden-white light. She spoke to her granddaughter: "I'm fine, don't worry about me. I have to leave you now. Take care of yourself." The next day, the mother found out that her grandmother had died during the night in a distant city.

Another woman had dreamed about an older male relative, someone she had not thought about or had contact with for a long time. In the dream, there was blood on her relative's chest. Unbeknownst to her, he had undergone open-heart surgery the previous day.

A different member of this small group had experienced recurrent dreams about her son. In these dreams her son, who was quite healthy at that time, appeared to have been seriously injured. The book club member saw herself in his hospital room and in that room a strong, mysterious voice would radiate throughout the room with these words: "He is being returned to you." She was confused because the boy in the dream, who she knew was her son, had much darker hair than her son's own hair. The dream recurred repeatedly for one month.

At the end of the month, her son was critically injured when his bicycle was struck by a car. In the hospital, this book club member told the concerned doctors that her son would recover. She knew this unequivocally; the voice had told her so. His head swathed in bandages, the boy slowly recovered. When the bandages were removed, the hair on his head, which had been shaved, grew in dark. The woman never had this dream again.

Another woman told the others about her two-year-old son who seemed to have an encyclopedic knowledge of facts to which he had never been exposed. "He must have been here before," she told her friends.

A woman's dentist, who was also her good friend, seemed to have a special talent for avoiding traffic accidents. One evening they, along with several other friends, were leaving a restaurant and beginning to cross the street. "Step back on the curb," he suddenly yelled and put up his arms in front of them, herding the group backwards. He had no idea why he was doing this. A few seconds later, a car careened around the corner and sped by recklessly, several feet in front of the group.

A few weeks after that incident, the dentist had been half-asleep in the passenger seat of his car as his wife was driving them home. He was not looking out the window, just dozing on and off. "Don't go when the light changes," the dentist mumbled when his wife braked for a stop light. "Someone is going to run the red light." He was still half-asleep and not looking out the window. She heeded his warning. A few seconds after the light changed, a car sped through the intersection across their projected path. They were both shocked, but alive.

While cleaning her house, one woman in the group was struck "out of the blue" by the clear and entirely convincing thought that an old friend of hers had just committed suicide. She had not thought of this friend for months and had no knowledge of any emotional problems or thoughts of self-harm. But the thought was so clear, so untinged by emotion, and so convincing, that it seemed like knowledge of a fact rather than an idle thought. It was true, she later learned. He had committed suicide on that very day.

These striking, intuitive experiences kept pouring out. Several more of the book club members related precognitive dreams. One typically knew who was calling her before she picked up the phone. Most had experienced strong déjà vu feelings, intuitive knowledge, and/or simultaneous thoughts and utterances with their husbands.

But what was perhaps even more striking was that in the twelve years the group had been meeting, these women had not shared most of the information about their psychic experiences. They were afraid of being considered "weird" or even "crazy." And yet these are normal women experiencing normal psychic phenomena. It is not weird or crazy to have these experiences—we all do. We just don't tell others about them, not even our families and closest friends.

In a sense, past life recall is just one of many directions the very common, very precious experience of intuition can take. A mind that is relaxed and focused in a light hypnotic state is often better able to tap the unconscious stores of intuitive guidance and wisdom than is the normal, "awake" mind, which receives random, spontaneous hunches. If you have ever had an intuitive experience, a hunch that has paid off or come true, you know how valuable and empowering such an experience can be.

The experience of past life recall often feels the same. It feels as if you are remembering, guiding, and healing yourself in a way you do not have to explain or prove. It simply happens; it flows. When you feel better as a result of your recall experience, whether a physical symptom has been alleviated, an emotional issue soothed, or you simply feel more confident and peaceful about your life and its direction—all very common results of past life therapy—you don't need to question the logical validity of the experience you have had. You *know* it has empowered you to improve the quality of your own life or to receive insight about yourself and others in a very tangible way.

Psychic, precognitive dreams are a particularly common example of an ability that we all have and that we all further develop. Soon after the state of Florida began a six-digit state lottery, an unusual psychic dream led a New Jersey man to win the $10.5 million prize. In an interview reported in the Florida newspapers, the winner said his daughter had appeared to him in a dream almost a month after her death, and she had prompted him to buy a lottery ticket.

"My daughter said, 'Why don't you play my numbers?' She said, 'I'd like to bring you a little happiness.' "

Her father, a sixty-one-year-old real estate agent, and other family members had come to Florida to try to recover from the sudden, tragic death of his twenty-three-year-old daughter who had died in a fall from a two-hundred-foot cliff in New Jersey several weeks prior to the dream. After awakening from this vivid dream, her father remembered that a New Jersey lottery ticket had been found in his daughter's car. He thought it very eerie, but he telephoned home for the numbers on her New Jersey ticket: 2, 6, 11, 14, 31, and 34. Early on the day that the weekly drawing was held, the father and mother, two daughters, and a son bought a single Florida lottery ticket with these numbers on it. The odds of winning are computed to be fourteen million to one. The family won.

"I got like a funny feeling," the father said. "I was surprised, but not surprised. It's hard to explain."

Later that month, a Homestead, Florida, man won $11.2 million by picking the numbers 1, 2, 3, 13, 28, and 48 in the Florida lottery. A fifty-eight-year-old body shop mechanic, he had never before bought a lottery ticket, not even in his native country, Cuba. But on the Tuesday night prior to Saturday's drawing, his dead mother appeared to him in a vivid dream and told him to buy a lottery ticket. He bought ten tickets at a nearby supermarket the next day. One of those ten turned out to be the winner.

Psychic, precognitive dreams are not only frequent but also quite real. I am aware of this not only from my recent research into psychic phenomena, but also from over twenty years of experience as a sleep and dream researcher.

The validation of near death experiences, or NDEs, through the research of many prestigious experts like Dr. Raymond Moody,

Dr. Elisabeth Kübler-Ross, Dr. Kenneth Ring, Dr. Melvin Morse, and others, also defines the intuitive, experience-based worldview in which past lives and recall of them seem logical and comfortable to both mind and intuition. It also highlights another very common human experience that many keep to themselves, and one that often parallels the findings of past life regression research.

Shirley is a sixty-five-year-old woman, one of the few survivors of an airplane crash in which more than 170 passengers were killed. Shirley was severely injured, with multiple fractures and damage to internal organs. She was found in marshy water, still belted into her seat, which had fallen out of the shattered fuselage of the plane.

Hospitalized in a trauma center, Shirley developed a fever of over 106 degrees, a potentially lethal level. She began to have convulsions, and she lapsed into a coma. She then had a cardio-respiratory arrest, and her breathing and heart rate ceased. Heroic efforts to resuscitate her appeared fruitless, but the medical team persisted.

During these efforts Shirley had a near death experience. Floating out of her body, she was met by a flock of white doves. They directed her toward a beautiful light in the distance. She felt wonderful. On the way, she turned around and saw the doctors and nurses frantically working on her body. She could see which bones in her body were broken as clearly as if she were looking at an X ray.

Turning back toward the beckoning light, she thought, "Oh, I wish the birds could talk."

At this point, she heard a voice coming from the light. The voice was calm and peaceful, and it was telling her that it was not yet her time.

Shirley protested, "But my body is crumpled. I don't want to go back to this pain."

The voice responded, "You have a message to bring back, and the message is that peace equals love, love equals wisdom."

Shirley was further told that she would help people by communicating this message.

Shirley returned to her body. The doctors were amazed. Fifteen minutes had passed since her heart had stopped beating, since she had last drawn a spontaneous breath. She later told everyone her message. Her family put posters around her room. "Peace, Love, Wisdom," the posters said.

Shirley heard the voice one more time, when her doctors told her that she would probably be permanently paralyzed, a paraplegic.

"No, I'm not!" she protested. "Come back in half an hour, and I'll prove it to you."

After they left, Shirley closed her eyes and pictured the light she had seen during her near death experience. Then she heard the voice again. "Your healing will come from within, from the inside out."

When the doctors returned at the appointed time, Shirley told them that her healing would occur from the inside out. She instructed them to watch her feet. Once again she closed her eyes and focused on the light. The skeptical doctors were completely taken aback when Shirley moved her foot. Since then, her recovery has been steady.

According to a Gallup survey, more than eight million Americans have had NDEs, including many young children. The accounts of these experiences are remarkably consistent and extremely well documented. Usually the person near death becomes detached from his or her body and "watches" the rescue and resuscitation efforts from some point above the body. Soon the person becomes aware of a bright light or a glowing "spiritual" figure or sometimes a deceased relative in the distance. Often, he or she hears sounds or music and floats down a tunnel toward the light or toward the figure. There is no pain. Instead, a feeling of intense peace and joy pervades the floating consciousness. Most people do not want to return to their bodies, but if their tasks, duties, and debts on earth are not yet completed, they are returned to their bodies, and once again become aware of pain and other physical sensations. Yet most are also aware that life does not end with the death of the physical body. Most never fear death again.

Raymond Moody, Jr., M.D., Ph.D., renowned author of *Life*

After Life, *Reflections on Life After Life*, and *The Light Beyond*, told me about some of the more than two thousand interviews he has conducted with people who have had NDEs. In his interviews, the subjects describe the typical experience of floating above their bodies. Many knew what the doctors and nurses who were attending to their bodies were going to say moments *before* the actual words were uttered. When patients tried to touch the doctors' or nurses' shoulders, their disembodied hands went right through the solid bodies of the medical team. There was no physical contact.

"They then open up to a sense of transcendent reality," Dr. Moody continued. "They feel totally permeated by love as they find the brilliant light, which in no way hurts their eyes."

One frequent characteristic of NDEs is a life review, a panorama of one's actions, behavior, and deeds that is somehow all displayed instantaneously, beyond time, and in brilliant color and three dimensionality. In addition, the life reviewer experiences the emotions of the people he has helped and hurt, loved and hated. One or several spiritual, godlike beings often accompany the life reviewer during the review.

One of Dr. Moody's subjects was a minister who had tended toward the fire and brimstone approach in his preaching. As the life review got underway, the preacher found himself experiencing one of his own vitriolic sermons from the perspective of a nine-year-old boy who was quaking with fear in his pew. The preacher's acquaintance with this boy prior to the NDE had been fairly casual, yet now he felt the full force of the boy's fear as well as the decidedly unspiritual effect of his sermon on the entire congregation.

It was then that the spiritual being who was observing the life review calmly commented, "I suspect you won't be doing *that* any more."

Recalled the minister to Dr. Moody, "I was very surprised that God was not interested in my theology!"

Dr. Melvin Morse, a Seattle pediatrician and author of *Closer to the Light*, has been carefully documenting NDEs in children since 1983, reporting more than fifty cases. Children who have had NDEs relate very similar experiences. They, too, describe leaving their bodies, entering a void, and being drawn to a bright, welcoming light. The impact of the NDE on children is equally as profound and transformative as it is on adults. The children learn that life has a real purpose. They "revere life and see the intricate connections throughout the universe." In a follow-up of his patients nearly eight years after the original interviews, Dr. Morse found that the children who had experienced NDEs had become exceptionally mature teenagers and forged excellent family relationships. They did not experiment with drugs, were not rebellious, and did not act out behaviorally or sexually.

Dr. Kenneth Ring, the founder and past president of the International Association for Near Death Studies, Professor of Psychology at the University of Connecticut, and the author of the excellent books *Life at Death* and *Heading Toward Omega*, as well as Dr. Morse, Dr. Moody, and I recently lectured at a medical conference in Los Angeles. The theme of the conference was near death and after death experiences. At the conference, Dr. Morse related that several children in his study had reported having overheard conversations among physicians and nurses during surgical procedures during the NDE, even though the children were unconscious under general anaesthesia at the time.

He also related the story of a child who had an NDE at the age of nine months. Later at the age of three and a half, the child attended a religious pageant and saw someone portraying Christ.

"That's not really Jesus," the boy objected. "I *saw* Jesus when I died!" Elaborating, the boy described how he had seen a tunnel with a "world of light" at the other end, where he could "run and double jump with God."

"This was his vision of heaven," Dr. Morse added. Dr. Morse also mentioned three or four children who told him that they "met souls in heaven waiting to be reborn" during their NDEs. "This bothered them," Dr. Morse commented, "because it seemed contrary to their religious training, yet they did meet these souls."

Dr. Moody told me about a case cited in the *Journal of Critical Care Medicine* of a child less than one year old who had nearly died but was revived at the last moment. Afterwards she showed signs of separation anxiety whenever she was near a tunnel. When the child was about three and a half, her grandmother became terminally ill, and the news of the impending death was delicately broken to the young girl.

"Oh, will Grandmother have to go through the tunnel to see God like I did?" she innocently asked.

In Dr. Ring's experience, religious orientation and background do not predispose people to NDEs. Anybody can have this experience, despite what their beliefs may be. He reiterated the finding that people experiencing NDEs lose the fear of death. "This does not happen with those near to death who don't have NDE's," says Dr. Ring. ". . . Almost every NDE'er develops a belief in God, even those who were atheists previously. There is a greater concern for life, for nature, for the environment. They are less judgmental about themselves and more compassionate for others. They are much more loving . . . it's love that matters . . . they have a heightened sense of purpose. They are more spiritual."

Dr. Ring also believes that as resuscitation technology continues its rapid advances and more people than ever begin to come back from the brink of death, the number of NDEs will increase and provide even more important new data.

Patients describing their actual deaths in past lives use the same images, accounts, and metaphors as do the children and adults who have had an NDE. The similarities are astounding, even though vivid past life death descriptions usually come from hypnotized patients with no previous familiarity with the NDE literature.

The similarity of the changes in values, perspective, and outlook on life that typically occur after the experience of an NDE and a past life recall is also very illuminating. You do not have to be hit by a truck or suffer a cardiac arrest to reap increased awareness or spirituality, decline in materialistic worries, the development of a more loving, peaceful nature, or any of the other benefits that past life regression and near death experience share. Members of both groups experience a dramatic lessening of the fear of death and express the new and certain conviction that love is what really matters.

In addition to fear of punishment or judgment by peers, an occasional third area of concern expressed by those interested in exploring past life recall is the question of validation. Is there any objective "proof" of past lives? Is there factual investigation into the veracity of the details of recalled past life memories? Sometimes this question arises in people who have already had a past life recall experience. Can all these details be true? They wonder. What if I made it up?

Ian Stevenson, M.D., Professor and Chairman Emeritus of the Department of Psychiatry at the University of Virginia, has collected and documented more than two thousand cases of children who have had a reincarnation-type experience. Many of these children exhibited xenoglossy, the ability to speak a foreign, often ancient language to which they had never been previously exposed. Usually very young, these children also knew specific and detailed facts about towns and families hundreds or thousands of miles distant and about events that occurred a decade or more ago. Half of these children came from the Western world, not India or Tibet or other areas in Asia where belief in reincarnation is common. Many of the details in these cases were carefully corroborated by Dr. Stevenson's research team.

Although my field is adult psychiatry, parents of children who appear to be experiencing a past life memory are also occasionally referred to me, so I have also had the opportunity to interview children with apparent past life recall.

The parents of one young boy sought me out to talk to me about their son's ability to speak French. The child had started speaking French in phrases and sentences when he was between the ages of two and a half and three. Could this be genetic memory of some sort, the parents wondered, since there was some French ancestry on one side of the family? However, neither parent could speak French, and the child had not been around any French-speaking people. No relatives, household caregivers, neighbors, or friends of the family spoke French.

After asking the parents more questions, I advised the little boy's parents that it was more likely that his xenoglossy was based on past life memory than it was on genetic memory. I told them that their son reminded me of Dr. Stevenson's children. It was certainly possible that, like them, he might be psychically tapping into a collective unconscious or stream of knowledge of all things, including history, languages, archetypal symbols, and past events. But, all in all, I felt that it was more likely that the boy had learned French in a prior life.

A distraught mother, an attorney by profession, was referred to me because her four-year-old daughter was behaving "strangely." Commitment to a psychiatric institution was even being considered. The child's "strange" behavior began after the mother bought some antique coins. She and her bright and hitherto very normal daughter had been sorting and playing with the coins when they came upon an odd, many-sided specimen.

The daughter immediately grabbed the coin and said, "I know this one. Don't you remember, Mommy, when I was big and you were a boy and we had this coin? Lots of them."

The daughter began to sleep with the coin and to talk fre quently about that other time. A psychologist friend of the family feared that the little girl might be psychotic. As I elicited further details about the case, I could confidently advise the family that the little girl was not psychotic; she was merely recalling a past life experience in a lifetime that she and her mother had once shared together. With reassurance and understanding, the daughter soon resumed her "normal" behavior, and the mother's anxiety disappeared.

These are not the only cases of this sort I and other researchers have in our files. Children such as these who spontaneously produce facts, details, languages, or other indications of past life recall are compelling examples of the reality of past lives. These children are too young to have studied the material they are presenting. They do not embellish or distort. This makes the information even more powerful.

I know of a three-year-old boy who can point out World War II vintage airplanes and can describe flying them when he was a man. He is able to provide some of the airplanes' specifications. How does he know this? I have heard about a little girl who remembers how to assemble rifles. Another describes in great detail the large sleigh that overturned on her when she was big.

There are many more examples of this phenomenon, thousands

in the literature. Just ask a three-year-old if he or she remembers when he or she was big. You may be amazed at the response.

As a trained psychiatrist, I instinctively compare the content of my patients' past life memories to the traditional psychoanalytic material of the dreams, with their attendant distortional and metaphorical content. In this way, I have been able to make my own discoveries about the issue of fantasy and metaphor versus actual memory in past life recall. I have also been able to compare the experience of past life regression with the traditional Freudian uncovering of childhood memories.

In my practice I have found that the fluid, living, seemingly multicolored mixture of actual experience, metaphor, and distortion that occurs in past life regression is very similar to the mixture that is found in dreams. In a past life regression session, my work is often to help pry apart these elements, interpret them, and find a coherent pattern to the whole tapestry, just as it is in a traditional psychoanalytic session, which might include childhood memories.

The difference is, again in my experience, that in dreams perhaps 70 percent of the dream content consists of symbol and metaphor, 15 percent consists of actual memory, and the last 15 percent of distortion or disguise. I have found that in past life recall, though, the proportions are usually rather different. Perhaps 80 percent of the past life experience will consist of actual memory, another 10 percent of symbol and metaphor, and the last 10 percent distortion or disguise. For instance, if you regress to your childhood in this lifetime and are asked to recall kindergarten, you may remember your teacher's name, the clothes you wore, the map on the wall, the friends you had, and the green wallpaper in the classroom. On further investigation, it may turn out that the wallpaper in your kindergarten classroom was actually yellow and that it was green in your first grade classroom. But this does not undercut the validity of the rest of your memory. Likewise, a past life memory may have an "historical novel" quality to it. That is, the important nucleus of truth may be filled out with fantasy, elaborations, or distortion, but the core of it will be a solid, accurate memory. The same phenomenon occurs in dream material and in regressions within the current lifetime. It is all grist for the mill. The truth is still there.

A traditional analyst might wonder whether a past life memory might be psychological fantasy. Is the past life memory a projection and embellishment of a childhood issue or trauma?

My experience and that of other therapists who have written to me about their cases tells me that it is actually the other way around. Memories, impulses, and energies from past lives seem to form or create the childhood pattern in this lifetime. It is simply another repetition or coming together of long, preexisting patterns.

Actually, this phenomenon of prior inputs from past lives surfacing in childhood and repeating once again is very similar to the concept of neurosis and repetition compulsion that Freud hypothesized (i.e., "hidden" traumas in the past that result in present symptoms, and which must be uncovered to relieve those symptoms). My only disagreement with traditional analysis on this particular point is that Freud's temporal stage was too small and limited, that it needs to be extended backwards beyond this lifetime to reach the root of some problems. Once that stage is enlarged, coherent, effective, and rapid therapeutic results usually occur.

As a therapist or a patient, you don't have to believe in past lives or reincarnation for past life therapy to work. The proof is in the pudding. As more than one fellow psychotherapist has said to me, "I still don't know if I believe in this past life stuff, but I use it, and it sure does work!"

4

Healing the Body by Healing the Mind

ELAINE IS A RESPECTED PSYCHOLOGIST IN THE MIAMI area. She came to me to see if past life therapy could alleviate a chronic physical condition. For years Elaine had suffered intermittent, excruciating pains in her neck, shoulders, and upper back. During the initial interview, I discovered that Elaine also had a lifelong terror of heights, a monosymptomatic or single-symptom phobia. This is how Elaine later described her experience during hypnosis and what happened to her life as a result:

"I saw a lot of darkness—blackness—and I realized that I was blindfolded. Then I saw myself from the outside. I was standing on top of a tower, one of those castle towers made of stone. My hands were tied behind my back. I was in my early twenties, and I knew that I was a soldier on the side that had lost the battle. Then I felt an excruciating pain in my back. I could feel my teeth gritting and my arms stiffen and my fists clench. I was being lanced, I could feel the lance in my back, but I was defiant, I wasn't going to scream. Then I felt myself falling, and felt the water of the moat closing around me.

"I've always been terrified of heights and drowning. When I came out of it I was still shaken, and I spent a couple of days in agony. I couldn't even touch my facial bones, the pain was so great. But the next morning when I woke up I thought, 'Something's different. Something's very different.' "

What was different was that Elaine's back pain and her fear of heights had disappeared.

In a subsequent session, Elaine vividly reexperienced a lifetime in medieval France. In this lifetime, Elaine had been an impoverished, dispirited, and hopeless male in his twenties. This man lacked the courage to be different, to speak out, to emerge from his rut and change his lot in life. Dispassionately, Elaine described the filthy brown rags that had been the man's only clothes. Eventually, the authorities wrongly accused Elaine of a crime she did not commit. But a scapegoat was needed, so Elaine was arrested and hanged in public. She went to the gallows grieving and mired in her hopelessness, almost relieved to be leaving her wretched existence.

After this session, her chronic neck pain disappeared. So did something else. As a result of her experiences in the French lifetime, Elaine was able to pinpoint a new area for emotional growth in the present. She saw that her experiences then had influenced her current reluctance to speak out and to take risks. Elaine decided to take the plunge. She risked her professional reputation by telling newspaper reporters and other therapists about her remarkable experiences in her past lives. And this time, instead of being hanged in public, she was congratulated.

Elaine's experience demonstrates how past life regression is expanding the repertoire of known techniques for accessing what has recently been dubbed "the mind-body connection."

Both old physical and old emotional cycles were broken in Elaine's therapy. Although she came to therapy for relief of physical symptoms, Elaine was not only able to rid herself of debilitating pain but also of a long-standing fear. As an additional bonus, she identified and pursued a new area of emotional growth for herself when she uncovered a block—the fear of speaking the truth—of which she had previously been unaware. During therapy, connections were made between Elaine's mind and body that interacted synergistically, playing off each other and opening new doorways of growth and wholeness until a new level of well-being emerged.

It is well known that the mind can strongly influence the body, causing symptoms, disease, and even death. All physicians know of hospital patients who gave up on life for one reason or another. Despite the best medical treatments and technology available, these patients wither away and die. Patients who possess a strong will to live usually fare much better. We are just now in the process of defining the physical mechanisms of "giving up" and "the will to live." These are the basic mechanisms of the mind-body connection, a connection that was made in a very healing way as Elaine shed her neck and back pain. In this chapter, we will explore many more examples of the mind-body connection as it is made during past life therapy and many of the different ways it can heal physical ailments.

Early data from Stanford University indicate that support groups significantly increase the quality *and* quantity of life in breast cancer patients. Harvard University researchers have found that some types of meditation can prolong life in the elderly. In his excellent book *Head First: The Biology of Hope*, Norman Cousins carefully documented work at UCLA and elsewhere that has helped to develop the new area of medical research known as psychoneuroimmunology, the interaction between the mind-brain and the immune system. Bernie Siegel, M.D., has also described mind-body correlations and the profound healing potential that is accessed through this linkage in his best-selling books *Love, Medicine and Miracles* and *Peace, Love and Healing*.

Research at Pennsylvania State University has shown that hypnosis can increase the quantity of certain white blood cells in the system. Numerous studies document correlations between improved athletic performance and visualization techniques. Many researchers and clinicians have used hypnosis to eliminate addictions to tobacco, food, and even to alcohol and hard drugs. Meditative techniques have also proved effective in many cases.

Past life therapy under hypnosis can also achieve some of these same results. I have done hundreds of therapeutic past life regressions since my first experiences with Catherine. I have seen that physical as well as psychological symptoms can rapidly resolve as a result of past life therapy, even without the use of medicines.

I am still not able to identify the exact mechanism of the physical cures that take place as a result of the therapy, although I do have some ideas. The cure might lie in the simple act of remembering and reexperiencing an initial trauma, just as the act of reexamining a childhood trauma during conventional psychotherapy results in an emotional cure. Or, the knowledge that the soul never dies, only the body does, could be the great healer. Healing may also occur as the patient acquires an understanding of the factors that precipitated the illness in the first place. Or, the secret may lie in a combination of all of these processes, all of which are typical of past life therapy.

Although I can only hypothesize about the reasons that past life recall heals, I can attest to the results of that recall. In my experience I have found that past life regression under hypnosis can be an important part of the treatment, amelioration, and even the cure of certain chronic symptoms and illnesses, especially those affected by the functioning of the immune system and those that may have a psychosomatic component.

Past life therapy is particularly effective in treating musculoskeletal pain, headaches that do not respond to medication, allergies, asthma, and stress-induced or immune-system-related conditions such as ulcers and arthritis. In some cases, it appears to improve cancerous lesions or tumors. Many patients of mine have been able to stop taking pain medication for formerly debilitating conditions after they experience past life therapy. It also resolves deep, underlying emotional issues as the relationship of the emotions to the physical discomfort and its past life source is revealed.

The medical exploration of this field is just beginning. However, it is safe to say that past life therapy must be seriously considered as a potent and cost-effective addition to the roster of effective holistic therapies, that is, therapies that concentrate not on alleviating a single symptom or condition but on healing the whole person, body and mind.

Wherever the secret lies, the therapeutic effects and benefits can be startling.

Jack is a forty-year-old cargo pilot who came to me for help with a cluster of physical and psychological symptoms. Physically, he suffered from migraines, gouty arthritis, and high blood pressure. Psychologically, Jack stored anger for weeks before suddenly venting his feeling in an intensity that approached rage. Jack also suffered from a very particular monosymptomatic phobia. Every morning as he buckled himself into his pilot's seat and taxied for take-off, he'd anxiously and repeatedly look out the window to make sure that his plane still had a right wing.

Having been an Air Force pilot for years before he became a commercial flier, Jack was an extremely seasoned and responsible pilot. He had never experienced any emergency situation that could have caused his current anxiety. Yet every morning when he woke up, all he could think about was whether the wing of his plane was going to fall off that day.

In therapy, Jack experienced a number of past lives in a combination of classical regression and the key moment flow process. In his first session, Jack recalled a life as a cowhand in the Old West. In that lifetime, Jack died when he was crushed by a falling boulder as he rode his horse through a mountain pass. As he relived the death experience, Jack recalled the suffocating feeling. As the regression continued, Jack moved into a different life and a second key moment.

He discovered that he had been a German air force pilot shot down by friendly fire over Germany in World War II. The friendly fire had blown away the right wing of his airplane. Jack died as the crippled craft plummeted to earth. As he reexperienced the death and the between-life stage that followed it, Jack also relived the terrible anger and frustration he had felt because of the mistake that had prematurely cost him his life and had forced him to abandon his young family.

After this regression process, Jack felt elated, as if a huge weight had been lifted from him. Now he had an explanation for the irrational anguish he had been experiencing in his present lifetime. Within two weeks, he and I both noticed that his wing phobia had entirely disappeared. Finally, he was able to get into the cockpit without casting a terrified glance out to the right side of his plane. His anger about the pointlessness of that death also helped him begin to understand more about the source of his frequent rages.

At Jack's second session, we decided to explore the origin of his gouty arthritis. Once in trance, Jack immediately slipped back into key moment flow regression and recalled a prior lifetime when he suffered severe bilateral knee injuries from running into a low fence. As a result of this accident, not only had he torn up both knees, but he had also endured serious infections, and eventually, atrophy of his lower legs. He never recovered fully and required care for the rest of his life. He had become angry and depressed and had an early demise.

Another connection between a current physical and emotional discomfort had been made.

Next Jack recalled an ancient lifetime in which an animal horn had penetrated his head, pierced the occipital lobe of his brain, and emerged from his body just underneath his right eye, the site of his present migraines.

Since that session Jack has not had another migraine. Although only time will tell if past life therapy has eliminated this chronic condition completely, there is a marked improvement in his level of well-being. His gout has also lessened. And much of Jack's anger has been replaced with peacefulness. His values have changed since he has experienced some of his previous lifetimes, and his perspective on life and its meaning has widened. Now that his fear of death has begun to erode, the things that previously angered or enraged him seem silly, small, irrelevant. This is a common result for many patients who have undergone past life therapy.

Selma is a forty-four-year-old woman who owns a printing business. Like Jack, Selma suffered from more than one chronic physical condition. Selma had a cancerous lesion on the vulva that had been removed several times but kept coming back. When she came to see me, she had been using a chemotherapy cream on the lesion with no effect. When we discussed her medical and psychological history, Selma related a number of physical and emotional challenges in her life. She suffered from allergies, skin rashes, and a history of stomach ulcers. At the age of eleven months she had badly burned the skin on her left thigh and had received one of the first skin grafts performed in America. Selma had numerous childhood surgeries on her thigh, accumulating a total of five hundred stitches. After an operation she underwent at the age of fourteen, Selma's body finally reacted to all the pharmaceuticals that had gone through her system by breaking out in an angry and painful red rash all over her body. After this, she became generally weakened, experienced more physical illnesses, and developed an intolerance to the sun. In addition, cancer ran in Selma's family. Her mother and her sister had died within the previous two years—her mother from brain cancer and her sister from cancer of the pancreas. And as a child, Selma had been sexually abused by an uncle.

Despite her many physical and emotional hardships, Selma came into therapy with hope and confidence that she could turn her life around. In her first regression, Selma saw herself as a dark-haired boy of thirteen, apparently a resident of a feudal village. Selma entered the lifetime at the moment of death, as armored men on horseback pillaged and destroyed her village. One soldier stabbed her in the chest with a sword and she died instantly. Selma's spirit immediately left her body. As it did, she felt a wonderful feeling of floating, a feeling of peacefulness and relief at leaving that earthly existence.

Selma then entered a centuries-ago lifetime in Holland and recounted how a relative living in that family's household had abused her sexually. She recognized that relative as the uncle who abused her in this life as well.

The factual details of these memories may have been hazy and fragmented, but the emotional content of the memories was very vivid and dramatic for Selma, particularly the memory of previous abuse. As we finished the session, Selma felt calm and composed, especially when reviewing the history of abuse with the Dutch man who was now her uncle. Selma experienced a great relief and clarity from being able to link these details together in a cause and effect pattern in her mind. As she discovered this pattern, she also seemed to free herself from some of the emotional residue of this traumatic childhood experience.

Eight days later, when Selma arrived for her next session, she reported that the cancerous condition had improved. The formerly recalcitrant lesion had shrunk dramatically and had become much less sensitive.

Selma also reported that in the interim she had experienced a dream about an aunt of hers who had burned to death at the age of sixteen, many years before Selma was born. Selma bears a close resemblance to this aunt, and family members tell her and photographs show her that they even have birthmarks in common. Since dreaming is also a common method of past life recall, Selma and I discussed this dream before proceeding with the session.

In the regression of that day, Selma recalled being a nurse on a large London hospital ward, probably in the nineteenth century. As she made her rounds, a soldier entered the room and shot her in the stomach and the chest. This session was extremely emotional for Selma, who relived the death experience before she floated upward. After this session, Selma's ulcer began to improve. Once again, she experienced what was for her the clarifying liberation of cause and effect.

Both Jack and Selma were able to make the mind-body connection through past life recall. Both of them discovered that past life therapy can not only trigger the amelioration of physical conditions but it can also heal emotional scars. In past life therapy, as the mind heals the body, the body can also help heal the mind.

Other physicians have contacted me to relate clinical vignettes about their patients' past life experiences. Dr. Robert Jarmon of

Spring Lake, New Jersey, wrote me because he had a patient who, like Catherine, spontaneously regressed to a traumatic past life experience.[1] This patient was also cured of her symptoms. This particular case of Dr. Jarmon's also illustrates how physical problems from past lives can carry over into the present lifetime.

Dr. Jarmon had been using hypnosis as a method of weight reduction for a Jewish woman in her mid-thirties. After two months of therapy, his patient began experiencing severe lower abdominal pain. Thinking that her symptoms could be caused by an ectopic pregnancy, a life-threatening condition in which the fetus develops in the fallopian tubes instead of the uterus, he sent her to a gynecologist. The area near her right ovary was tender and swollen. Her menstrual periods had stopped, but the woman was not pregnant. All tests were negative.

Five months passed, and her symptoms persisted. During a hypnosis session, Dr. Jarmon, working with her on a psychological problem, instructed her to "go back to the time when your problem began." Her subconscious mind chose the gynecological problem.

He was flabbergasted when the woman described a scene from the Middle Ages in which she was nineteen years old and five months pregnant. She was about to die because "the baby was out of place." A priest and a doctor were present.

"She started speaking to me as if I were the priest," Dr. Jarmon reported. "I answered her. Then she repeated the Catholic Act of Contrition, word for word. Her breathing became shallow and she described her death."

But the woman is Jewish. When she came out of hypnosis, she did not recognize any of the words she had just uttered. She had never heard of the Act of Contrition, which Catholics use to atone for their sins. Her abdominal pain was gone. Her menstrual periods came back that evening, and that pain has not recurred.

[1] Dr. Jarmon also wondered if he could be the Robert Jarrod mentioned in *Many Lives, Many Masters*. While in a hypnotic trance, Catherine had told me that "Robert Jarrod" needed my help. I had no idea who Robert Jarrod was, nor how I could help him. Catherine was never able to supply any other information about him. Because she spoke in a whisper, I could only guess at the spelling of his name, and I tried to reproduce it phonetically. I am still intrigued. Maybe she had really said "Jarmon."

The spiritual component of past life therapy is also a great healer. As patients personally experience that they do not die when their bodies die, they realize that they, in fact, have a divine nature that transcends birth and death. The will to live, to be healed, and the faith that healing can and will take place often increase with it. Patients learn of the higher power within all of us that helps us orchestrate our lives to learn and to reach our godlike potential. They become less anxious, more relaxed. More of their energy can be directed toward the healing process and away from fear and suffering.

Past life therapy also seems to develop those traits of hardiness that seem to correlate with good health, including increased resistance to the debilitating effects of chronic illnesses and with strong immune functioning. It promotes happiness, peacefulness, and the tendency to accept obstacles as challenges and adventures. Patients who have undergone past life therapy to alleviate physical problems become more hopeful, and they live life more joyously and fully. They are more independent. They sleep better. Their depression lifts.

Dana came to a small workshop of mine complaining of a problem with her throat. Her throat felt "lumpy," she often choked, she had frequent respiratory infections, and she was losing her voice. In a group regression, she had a vividly dramatic memory of a male lifetime in the Italian Renaissance in which she had been stabbed in the throat, although she did not know why she had been murdered.

After this workshop experience, Dana made an appointment to see me privately. In the office, she related a history of being abused by both parents when she was a child. In hypnosis she again relived the Italian Renaissance death experience, and this time it became less dramatic. This is a typical reaction. Each time a past life is relived, the emotion becomes less intense, and the possibility of gaining insights from the experience is increased.

During this session, Dana learned that she had been murdered because she had known an important secret that others were afraid she would reveal. She had not revealed this information, fearing the consequences of speaking out. This time, Dana continued on to the life review stage after the death was reexperienced. Here she learned that she will experience throat constriction and put herself in danger if she does not speak the truth.

At her next session, Dana entered a life that appeared to take place on a Pacific island, possibly Polynesia or Hawaii. In that lifetime, Dana was a young woman with psychic abilities who was absorbed with tribal dancing. She was so absorbed that when she was left to watch a fire, she neglected it. When the fire burned out of control, she neglected to warn her people. The community she lived in was consequently destroyed. One of the victims was the woman who is her abusive mother in this lifetime. The theme had recurred. She had not communicated when she should have.

After these sessions, Dana's throat symptoms improved. Moreover, she gained an important, wider perspective about her mother. She was able to step back and see her mother as someone with whom she had been playing different roles in many lifetimes. As a result, she was able to detach from the tyranny of the abusive situation in the present lifetime, one that had wounded her so deeply. This part of her past began to assume a smaller and less influential role in her present. Dana also learned that she needs to speak the truth, no matter what, whether about her abusive situation or a minor life detail, that secrecy is harmful and hurtful.

The healing process that occurs during regression sessions is not always all-encompassing. Sometimes it is a simple matter of discovering the past physical origin of a present physical pain. A patient who does not need to explore complex emotional issues as part of the source of current physical discomfort will not do so during past life therapy. The healing can be simple and direct.

Chronic headaches are one of several conditions that respond particularly well to past life therapy. My wife, Carole, had been suffering premenstrual migraine headaches for many years. Every month like clockwork she would develop severe and disabling migraines, and she would often have to rest for a day or two until the pain and nausea subsided. In addition, a neck injury suffered in an automobile accident in 1976 not only exacerbated these headaches but also resulted in a similar migraine whenever she served a ball on the tennis court or made certain types of overhead movements with her right arm. The menstrual periods and the overhead motions invariably precipitated a migraine headache. Gynecologists and neurologists had told her that nothing could cure the problem, that only medication could ease the pain.

In the late summer of 1988, Carole had a series of particularly severe migraine headaches. Meditation, which sometimes lessened her pain, did not alleviate the severity of these headaches. She did not want to use narcotic-like drugs, so she made an appointment with a hypnotherapist to learn hypnotic techniques to deal with the pain. I had once tried to hypnotize Carole, but our closeness interfered with the distance needed in a therapist-patient relationship.

Carole had no expectations as she dreamily drifted into a trance state. After a period of relaxation and stress reduction, the therapist told her to ask herself why she was getting these headaches. A scene flashed before her eyes, and Carole suddenly watched herself running from a mob. She was a poor peasant male who was wearing filthy brown or black burlap clothes. The time was about one thousand years ago, and the scene was taking place somewhere in Central Europe. The mob caught up to her and began to club her, punishing her for unacceptable beliefs and heresies. A blow caught her above the left eye, the very spot where the pain from the migraine was most severe. Suddenly, in the hypnotherapist's office, Carole began to experience that stabbing pain over the left eye, a pain that rapidly spread to the entire left side of her head. Carole knew that she had died as a result of this clubbing. The therapist said, "You no longer need this pain; let it go." Immediately the pain disappeared.

There is no way to prove whether this was an actual past life memory or not, but Carole has not had an incapacitating migraine headache since that session. Fantasies and daydreams do not cure such severe symptoms. Past life therapy very often does.

Tricia was a twenty-eight-year-old engineer suffering from temporomandibular joint pain (TMJ), migraines, and a stiff neck. She recalled a death experience somewhere in a valley of Asia Minor in the year 893 B.C. In that lifetime she had been a man living a very peaceful and happy life, which she related to me in great detail. When I asked her to look at her feet, she described the sandals she was wearing. Next Tricia switched to another ancient lifetime, again male, in which she lived in a cave in Greece. This time when I asked her to describe her footwear, Tricia was wearing sandals of a completely different style. Tricia described a warrior standing over her with a spear. The warrior then speared her face.

As she reexperienced her death, Tricia told me the pain she had felt then was very similar to the migraine pain she experiences in this lifetime.

Tricia's neck stiffness and TMJ improved gradually and significantly after her regression, and her migraines have diminished, freeing her from the need to take medication for them.

This ability to be free from medicines can be as important as relief from the pain itself. Alberto, a physician specializing in radiology, had suffered from severe back pain and spasms for many years. Medical treatments had been unsuccessful in alleviating the excruciating pain. If Alberto had not had such a strong and positive personality and character structure, he could have easily succumbed to the addictive potential of the potent pain-killing medicines he required during flare-ups of his back pain.

Falling into a relaxed trance state, Alberto uncovered two past lives where he had suffered mortal injuries to his back. One was especially revealing. In this lifetime as a soldier several hundred years ago, Alberto recalled dying painfully on a European battlefield, and he reexperienced the numbing pain of his fatal wound. The location of this wound corresponded exactly to the source of his current lower back pain. After the regression, Alberto's back pain and spasms quickly improved.

Once again, mind and body had come together to facilitate healing. In Alberto's case, the result was more focused than in many of the other cases described above. Alberto came to have physical pain relieved, and he achieved his goal.

Although Alberto's results were very specific, they still influenced his life in a broad way. As a result of his past life therapy, Alberto was able to stop taking the powerful painkillers that had previously provided his only source of relief.

Betty was another patient who used regression therapy to end a dependence on medicines. Betty had been afflicted with asthma, allergies, and a weakness of her respiratory system since childhood. She required injections of adrenaline and doses of steroids and other medicines to control her attacks and symptoms. She seemed destined to live out the rest of her life plagued by these terrible bouts of asthma, dependent on medicines just to breathe. Betty's personality and life circumstances were different from Alberto's, and she had even become addicted to a nasal decongestant spray.

During regression therapy, Betty began choking and gasping for air. She related to me that she was being burned at the stake, sometime in the late Middle Ages. The smoke was overpowering; her lungs were being seared. Betty eventually floated out of her body, hovering above it and the crowd, to watch the gruesome destruction of her body in the flames.

After the regression session, her asthma improved almost immediately. I still marvel that such a severe, life-paralyzing, lifelong symptom could resolve literally overnight. It seems miraculous to me. Yet it did, along with most of her other allergies. After her experience, Betty quickly stopped using the addictive decongestant, experiencing only minimal rebound stuffiness. Not only did the affliction disappear, but the quality of her life improved immeasurably. Her fears diminished markedly.

Betty is not the only patient of mine who had healed herself or himself of chronic allergies or respiratory problems through recall of a death experience that included the searing of the lungs or suffocation. Like migraine headaches, asthma, respiratory infections, and allergies are physical conditions in the current lifetime that seem to have origins in suffering experienced in previous lifetimes. Past physical trauma seems to leave present physical residue.

Lacey was a high school teacher in her late forties with a long history of asthma and a fear of water. During our first session, she went directly to a death scene and found herself as a girl of eight or nine falling off a cliff and drowning. Lacey recalled how her most vivid experience of this drowning was a sensory one, of the coldness and surprising depth of the water. Very quickly, she began to float peacefully out of her body. Next, Lacey found herself recalling a life in which she had been a young slave girl of eleven or twelve in the ancient Near East. In this lifetime, her task was to help make bricks out of wet hay or straw. Lacey died at this age when a wagon of wet straw fell over on her, and she suffocated. As she recalled the death experience, Lacey related the agony, panic, and terror she felt when she found that she could no longer take a breath. This death experience was quite different from the first one. Since that session, her asthmatic condition improved considerably, to the extent that for the first time in her life she was able to go through an entire allergy season without taking any medications or experiencing any symptoms.

Anne, an intensive care unit nurse, alleviated her respiratory allergies with a past life memory that began to well up spontaneously during a vacation. Anne was exploring Paris for the first time with her husband when she began to feel anxious for no apparent reason. As her anxiety increased, she also realized that she somehow also knew her way around the historic district she was exploring. She could easily navigate its twists and turns. Suddenly, as she turned a corner and looked down at the small square at the end of the street, Anne had an experience of déjà vu. She saw herself being burned at the stake several hundred years ago for her psychic healing abilities.

Anne subsequently came into the office for hypnosis therapy to explore this experience. In the structured therapy setting, Anne remembered the scorching heat and how she had died inhaling the thick, suffocating smoke that arose with it. Anne's recurrent respiratory allergies had not been her impetus for entering therapy; the spontaneous memory had. But this registered nurse later reported to me that her allergies had shown a marked improvement as a result of exploring this memory.

Another of Dr. Jarmon's patients, a fifty-one-year-old female executive, began hypnosis to trace the origin of her respiratory problems. Her name was Elizabeth.

"Now I want you to go to an old scene," Dr. Jarmon instructed Elizabeth. "I want you to go back to the first time you had that problem where you couldn't breathe, the feeling you couldn't catch your breath. As you see that scene, describe what you see."

Elizabeth began to tremble. She grimaced.

"There it is," Dr. Jarmon said. "I want you to look down at your feet. What are you wearing on your feet?"

"Dark shoes," she reported, in a child's voice. "Old lady's shoes."

The doctor probed further. "Where are you? What are you doing?"

"Sewing. But I know what's going to happen. There's going to be a fire." Elizabeth stammered and began coughing. Her breathing became rapid and shallow. "Smoldering . . . the rags over there in the corner."

Elizabeth described herself as a sixteen-year-old girl named Nora who lived in Sterling, Massachusetts, in 1879. Nora worked in a shirt factory. She was deaf, could not speak, and wore braces on her legs. She had been working in this factory since age twelve.

"Smoke . . . flames!" she coughed. "They are trying to put it out . . . they are hitting it. They're beating it. Someone threw water on it, but there's not enough water," she cried. Her breathing became very labored.

"Everybody's trying to get out," she sputtered.

"How about you? Are you trying to get out?" Dr. Jarmon asked.

"I can't," she answered. "They won't help me!"

"Why do you need help?"

"I can't walk . . . I have braces on my legs," Elizabeth cried, gasping for air. "They don't even see me. I'm there. I can't breathe. I can't stand it any more," she gulped.

Suddenly she went limp. After several silent and tense minutes, Dr. Jarmon asked her to describe the scene.

"Is the fire still raging?" he asked.

"Yes . . . but I'm resting . . . I'm dead . . . still sick . . . have to rest. Some need more rest than others. But it's okay. Now it's peaceful."

Elizabeth's respiratory problems disappeared after she reexperienced her death in the fire. She lost her lifelong fear of suffocating. Her values and her life changed dramatically.

All these cases and so many others show that there is more than increased strength deriving from the clear awareness of our inherent divinity and the higher power guiding each of us throughout our lives. There is more than the immune system boost from living life more joyously and completely, with hardiness and power. There is also recovery through understanding the true root causes of our symptoms, our fears, our impairments, our dependencies.

When the core reasons are seen and experienced, understood and resolved, the symptoms disappear. The illnesses improve. The splinter has been removed, and the pain is gone. The recurrent drama has finally ended, and the dance is over. There is no need to project, to defend, to anaesthetize, to use drugs, to be sick any more.

Perhaps this is why therapy conducted in this state, from this higher perspective, seems to be extremely effective. Learning occurs at a highly accelerated pace. Sometimes regression to childhood or to a past life is not even necessary. When therapy is done in a relaxed, meditative, "higher" state, learning, acceptance, assimilation, and improvement frequently take place quite rapidly.

The benefits of the "higher" state can be experienced in forms of therapy other than past life therapy. I have been incorporating some of its elements into traditional psychotherapy with some of my nonregression patients. I tell the patient to gently close his or her eyes and to take a few deep breaths, letting the body completely relax. We then converse therapeutically. The patient's vision is directed inward instead of outward. There are many fewer distracting sights and thoughts. Concentration is focused. The subconscious mind can be accessed and influenced in a positive, healing manner.

Frequently the patient experiences visual images that accompany the thoughts and emotions we are reviewing. These images seem to be very important and to be directly related to the symptoms or blocks the patient is experiencing. We discuss and integrate the meaning of these images, whether they are symbolic or actual memory fragments. Learning and clinical improvement are enhanced.

Evelyn has a particularly virulent form of premenopausal breast cancer, which has metastasized. Only two years before her own diagnosis was made, Evelyn experienced a severe grief reaction to her sister's death from cancer. When she came to see me, Evelyn had already been through numerous courses of radiation and chemotherapy. She had undergone a surgical menopause in order to negate hormonal influences on her cancer. Evelyn was despondent and losing hope, and her clinical course was heading downhill.

In a hypnotic state, we patched up some old family problems. In this hypnotized, superconscious state, Evelyn met her deceased sister. They talked, hugged, expressed their love for each other, and knew that they would "always" be bonded together in some way. Evelyn realized that her sister was not dead, that she had merely left her body behind.

Next Evelyn visualized lights like laser beams zapping her tumors, cleansing her body, adding a turbocharge to her immune system. Spirit guides came to help with the laser zapping.

Evelyn began to improve. She gained weight and went into remission. She became more hopeful, fighting to live. Her grief and depression rapidly disappeared. She felt joy and peace reenter her life.

Was her improvement due to the hypnosis and the healing

visualizations? The time course suggests a correlation. There were also other factors. Her oncologists were able to use higher amounts of chemotherapy medicines because she was feeling better and stronger. Perhaps the added medicines were the crucial factor. Yet, without the hypnosis and visualizations, she could not have tolerated the increased doses of the powerful chemotherapy drugs.

In a study reported in *The Lancet*, the prestigious British medical journal, medical researchers found that a combination of diet, exercise, and the practice of stress reduction techniques can *reverse* blockages in coronary artery disease. Changes in diet and exercise alone were not sufficient to reverse heart disease. Stress reduction was a necessary factor, more important than originally believed.

Dr. Claude Lenfant, a researcher at the National Heart, Lung, and Blood Institute in Bethesda, Maryland, stated that these lifestyle changes "can begin to reverse even severe coronary artery disease after only one year, without the use of cholesterol-lowering drugs." Relaxation techniques are very important.

"This finding suggests that conventional recommendations . . . may be enough to prevent heart disease but not to reverse it," commented Dr. Dean Ornish, who coordinated the study.

In another study of more than one thousand heart attack victims, researchers from Stanford University presented a report at the International Congress of Behavioral Medicine in Uppsala, Sweden. They found that anxiety, fearfulness, hostility, and anger are psychological traits that predispose people to second heart attacks. Interestingly, anxiety and fearfulness seem to be more harmful to women while hostility and anger are more harmful to men.

Relaxation, visualization, imagery, and regression are used in order to eliminate stress, tension, fears, and phobias, in a holistic way—the health ramifications seem endless.

We need more research into the mind/brain/immune system/body continuum. How do attitudes and particular states of mind help to prevent, ameliorate, and sometimes cure addictions, chronic illnesses, infections, cancers, heart disease, autoimmune disorders, and other diseases?

It has been my experience, and that of many other doctors as well, that regression therapy and hypnotic visualization can transform the mind to reach these healing states. These methods can be used in conjunction with traditional medical approaches and medicines. They are not mutually exclusive, by any means, as the treatment of many of the patients in this chapter demonstrates.

Here is one final example. Frances is a woman in her mid-forties who came to me to work on some relationship issues. She had also been recently diagnosed as having two masses in her right breast. The breast masses had been definitively identified as solid, striated masses, not as the fluid-filled cysts that can come and go at different stages of the menstrual cycle. I conducted the preliminary interview, noting Frances's psychological and physical history, and we made a second appointment.

On the day of her second appointment, Frances arrived in an agitated state. Since our first session, she had gone to see an oncologist about her breast lumps, which were possibly cancerous. The oncologist had tried to perform a needle biopsy on the breast masses, but Frances had fainted. Her doctors had decided they wanted to remove the two masses surgically, and Frances was very anxious, not only about the possibility that they would prove to be cancerous, but also because she had once had a bad experience under general anaesthesia similar to a near death experience and was afraid she would repeat it.

During our session we did visualization work with healing lights, just as Evelyn and I did and as many other patients have done. I gave Frances the audio tape with a relaxation and healing meditation and suggested that she do the same work at home. We made a third appointment for the following week.

Frances had quite an astounding story to tell during the third appointment. She had arrived to have her surgery as planned early on a Monday morning. As part of the preparation for surgery, her radiologist had run a final breast X ray.

When he looked at the film, the lumps that had been present on a previous workup taken only three days before were completely gone.

The startled doctor immediately scheduled Frances for an emergency mammogram.

Same result. No lumps.

As Frances lay on the operating table with an IV in her arm, her radiologist announced the results to her surgeon while also showing the man the data.

Frances's surgeon told her radiologist that he wanted to operate anyway, on the basis of the last set of X rays.

The two physicians proceeded to have a disagreement right in front of their sedated patient, who was waiting on the table to have surgery. The surgeon was recalcitrant, and refused to believe the new evidence even though his highly qualified associate, the radiologist, saw that two separate and highly reliable tests had shown that Frances's breast lumps had disappeared.

Finally Frances took matters into her own hands.

"There aren't any lumps there," she said. "So I'm going home."

Later, Frances sent me the following message in a holiday greeting card:

> Thank you for the meditation regression tape. I am "living proof" that the healing light works! I experienced a miracle today when I went into the hospital for my lumpectomy. Both lumps had disappeared from Friday to Monday. I've been 100% healed!! (amazing, powerful stuff, that "white light")
>
> Now all of my friends and relatives are believers, too, and want copies of the tape! All the skeptics and doubters, including my husband, are beginning to listen to the value of meditation, etc. I will always remember this Hanukkah as the "turning point" in my life. And I will always celebrate the "Festival of Lights" with a new meaning! P.S. I look forward to even more wonderful experiences toward HEALTH.

Frances's experiences may be much less uncommon than people think.

The transformational power of the mental attitudes induced by hypnotic past life regression and visualization can be of real practical use to traditional medical practitioners. Here are safe and strong healing forces, forces with no side effects because these forces are basically spiritual and intuitive in nature. This is truly holistic medicine.

5

Healing Troubled Relationships

DAN, A BUSINESS EXECUTIVE IN HIS LATE THIRTIES, was seeing me for therapy for several reasons, one of which was his passionate yet turbulent love relationship with Mary Lou. He is an intense, intelligent, and idealistic Italian-American from Boston's North End. Mary Lou is from South Carolina, from a very different culture and religious background. The two started with a strong, immediate, and passionate attraction to each other. That was not their problem.

The problem began with her flirting. After Mary Lou had a drink or two, her usually tightly controlled behavior would disappear. Then she would enjoy hugging their male friends, touching their hair, rubbing their necks, kissing them when arriving and leaving, and sometimes even spontaneously in between. Yet this was the extent of it. There was never any additional sexual acting out. There was never an affair, only flirting, and this behavior always occurred in public.

Dan would go crazy. He would rage, yell at Mary Lou, and

demand that she respect herself more and act more properly. He could barely control his anger. The extent of his emotional reaction transcended the concept of macho or male pride and possessiveness in his culture. Dan's rage transcended any previous personal reactions with other women. He had been married once and divorced, had dated a lot, and had had several long-term relationships, but he had never experienced anything like this rage with any of the other women.

For several weeks Dan and I talked about his anger. Then, on one particular Thursday afternoon, he appeared for his appointment with seething anger. She had done it again! At a dinner party, Mary Lou had flirted with one of their male friends. Dan had felt like "breaking her neck," and Mary Lou was frightened.

Here were two otherwise sophisticated, mature professionals, but she could not stop drinking, flirting, or provoking him, and he would always become a raging bull whose reaction was very disproportionate to her "crime."

For thirty minutes Dan and I talked about the party, about her behavior and about his. As the scene replayed itself in his mind, Dan could not control his anger.

"Why does she continue to do this?" he raged, pounding the desk. "Is she trying to destroy the relationship?"

Significantly, Mary Lou was willing to convert to his religion for the sake of the relationship. And they were planning a wedding.

We were getting nowhere with our talking. Ventilating his anger, fears, and other feelings did not help because the reservoir of his emotions was much too full. He was willing to go along with a suggestion I made.

"Let's try to go back to the real source, the root, of your relationship. Perhaps you had a girlfriend like Mary Lou. Perhaps there is something deeper. Let's find out."

Dan allowed himself to be hypnotized, and soon he was in a deep hypnotic trance. I told him to allow his mind to remember the roots of their relationship problem, to go back to the causes.

I never know what to expect when this nondirective approach is used. No matter how many patients I have regressed in this manner, I still get surprised and humbled by what comes out.

His body, which in the trance had become very relaxed and peaceful, again became tense. He seemed to be listening to something.

"I can hear my cousin," this highly successful executive whispered. "I can see him! He's dressed in a white robe and has a dark beard. My uncle is with him. They are talking to me."

This man's cousin and uncle had both died many years ago.

"They're telling me to let her go! They're saying, 'Let her go. She needs to develop, to overcome her attitudes and handicaps. But this is for her sake, for her development, not for yours or for your comfort. This is a test of love. Then she can come back to you, when she has overcome her negative traits.' "

There was more.

"We will now show you," Dan's relatives said.

Suddenly Dan watched with amazement and horror as a series of past lives with his lover flashed before his mind's eye.

"I'm stabbing her with a long dagger!" Dan observed miserably. "She has been unfaithful to me, and I have killed her in anger." This occurred around the seventh or eighth century and he was a warrior and an early follower of Mohammed.

Dan had also killed Mary Lou in two other ancient lifetimes. In a few others he had left her, usually in dire or dangerous situations. Thus, he had already killed her three times and had abandoned her several times, and yet Mary Lou kept springing back into a new life like a phoenix, ready to repeat the same script once again.

All in all, Dan found Mary Lou and this repetitive pattern in at least six lifetimes. These were only the lifetimes in which he, always the male, killed or rejected her, always the female. In subsequent past life regressions, we learned that the two had also been together in other family or friend or enemy relationships with the sexes and roles sometimes reversed.

Dan's rage and anger vanished completely. In less than an hour he felt more love and tenderness toward Mary Lou than he had been able to feel and express since the very beginning of their relationship in this lifetime.

Dan later told Mary Lou about the regression session and tried to "let her go." She would not go. She wanted to do the necessary work from within the relationship, without physically severing the bond. Dan realized that "letting go" did not necessarily mean "sending away." There are many ways to let go.

Dan also realized, as these and other past life patterns were revealed, that his "warrior" needed more of the strength that comes from love, compassion, awareness, and understanding. He needed the strength derived from wisdom, hope, and faith, and less of the pseudo-strengths of anger and rage.

He also realized that his cousin and uncle were still alive, even though their bodies had died. He now knew, in his heart and his bones, that he, too, would never die.

Within a year Mary Lou and Dan married. That was two years ago from the time of this writing. Their problem pattern has never recurred. He has stopped behaving in an accusatory way toward her, and she has stopped provoking him. Their communication is far better than it was in the golden days when they met because they have both learned an important lesson about anger. They have seen how destructive negative patterns can be, and how long lasting. Now, as soon as either of them senses a problem, no matter how small, they discuss it and try to resolve it. As a couple, Dan and Mary Lou truly have an ability to communicate joyfully, deeply, and intimately.

Some of our more difficult and challenging life experiences occur in the context of relationship and families. And so do many of our most fulfilling and loving ones. We live in our bodies, and we express ourselves through our relationships. This is how we human beings communicate. It is our primary method of learning and evolving.

Through my experience I have learned that many of the severe and chronic conflicts therapists see in couples therapy, marital therapy, and family therapy actually have their root causes in prior lives. Therapy that explores other lifetimes in addition to the present one can resolve relationship conflicts that prove to be resistant to the usual therapeutic techniques, as Mary Lou's and

Dan's were. When the search for the root of the problem or its treatment is expanded beyond the limited time span of the current relationship, much suffering can be minimized, or even avoided. Often, the anger, hatred, fear, and so many other negative emotions and behaviors manifesting in the current life relationship may actually have had their beginnings centuries ago.

Diana, a wealthy forty-year-old woman from Philadelphia, came to see me because of her chronic depression. As therapy progressed, I became convinced that a tumultuous and perpetually hostile relationship with her daughter was the root of this woman's unhappiness.

My patient had experienced an instantaneous dislike of this daughter dating from the first moment she held the newborn baby in her arms. Diana had not experienced these upsetting emotions at the birth of any of her other three children. Far from it. Joy and elation had been the hallmark of their births. Diana was perplexed by the instant and lingering anger and revulsion she had felt toward Tamar, who was now eighteen. By the time Diana entered therapy, the two had been arch enemies for nearly two decades. Their relationship was punctuated by frequent, violent arguments that were usually set off by something trivial.

During regression therapy, Diana related that she had suddenly gone into hemorrhagic shock and nearly died just before Tamar's birth. Diana remembered floating out of her body and watching her husband panic and run out to get the doctors. She had then experienced a classic near death episode.

After this session, I thought that the relationship might improve. Perhaps the patient had nurtured an unconscious or subconscious hatred of this child because the birth had nearly killed her. This regression memory alone might have provided the catharsis necessary to release those negative emotions.

At her next session, however, Diana reported that life with Tamar remained as stormy as ever. We tried regression therapy again. This time we were more successful. Diana's memories revealed that this lifelong animosity, felt equally by mother and daughter, had its source not in the birth experience, but in a past life. In the lifetime in question, Diana and Tamar had not been related. They had been arch rivals for the same man's affections. And the man in question was now Diana's husband and Tamar's father in this lifetime!

Clearly, the arch rivals were still battling it out in their current incarnations.

Diana and Tamar's relationship improved somewhat after she had this memory of their past life competition. Diana did not tell Tamar about the episode since she simply didn't feel comfortable about sharing this unusual experience. But when Tamar underwent a past life regression with a different therapist in another state, she regressed *to the very same past life with the very same details*. At this point, Diana was shocked enough to share her own experience with her daughter.

With this startling and illuminating new perception, their relationship finally transcended the fixed script of endless competition and hostility. Diana and Tamar are now good friends.

On a sunny, humid October morning, I drove to my office after helping to get my daughter, Amy, off to school. On the way out, I hugged Carole good-bye.

"Don't forget to work on the relationship chapter," Carole reminded me. We had been talking about intimate relationships and couples therapy on and off over the weekend, discussing the effects of past life connections on current life relationships. Carole knew I had left some time at the end of the day to begin writing down our thoughts and conclusions.

At eleven, my only "new" patient of the day came in. She had somehow convinced my secretary to bump her to the top of my waiting list, and the day of her appointment had finally arrived. After she left, I reminded myself that there are no coincidences.

Martine, a thirty-year-old mother of two, stated that her only problem was a "terrible" seven-year marriage. Her childhood had been happy, and her relationship with her parents was still wonderful. Her children, a four-year-old daughter and a two-year-old son, were joys to her. Martine liked her house and had many good friends. She enjoyed her job in a dentist's office.

However, Martine's husband, Hal, was constantly critical, demanding, and negative. Hal found fault with everything Martine did, and he never lost an opportunity to criticize or demean her. He was like a lead weight to her, an anchor around her neck, yet she persisted in trying to make the marriage work. They had already separated several times, twice during her second pregnancy. Martine had not wanted to become pregnant that time, but Hal had "pushed and pushed" for it. And then he had left her. Eventually he returned, guilt-ridden, but soon left her again. Martine seemed to passively accept the situation, Hal's behavior, and his ultimata. Individual and couples psychotherapy had not improved the marital discord at all.

Several weeks prior to our session in the office, Martine had attended a workshop I presented in Miami. During the workshop I taught a group of about two hundred people how to visualize and how to experience regressions while in a hypnotized state. Twice I had taken the entire group on a past life journey. Their eyes were closed and their bodies were entirely relaxed as my voice guided them to remember details from childhood and then even further back to memories from a previous lifetime.

Martine had reached a state of deep relaxation during these exercises. She felt serene and peaceful. She remembered herself as a child in this lifetime, but she went no further. She had no past life memories at all. She saw nothing.

Martine had bought an audiotape to use at home. The tape is of my voice conducting relaxation and regression exercises. (A modified written version of this tape is found in Appendix A of this book.) When Martine listened to the tape at home, she was able to relax deeply, and sometimes even fell asleep. But she still had no success recalling past life scenes.

In my office I took Martine's medical and psychological histories and then hypnotized her to a deep level. Unlike her experience during the workshop or while listening to the tape, she could now answer my questions, and I could guide her more carefully and specifically. When I asked Martine to find a pleasant childhood memory, she moved easily back to her fifth birthday.

"I see my parents and my grandparents. There are lots of presents around." Martine was smiling as she recalled this memory. Clearly, it was a very happy one. "My grandmother made the chocolate cake she always makes. I can *see* it."

"Open some presents and see what gifts you got," I suggested. She was delighted as she opened some of the brightly wrapped gifts and found clothes, a new doll, and much more. The joy of the five-year-old girl was evident in her beaming face. I decided to move on.

"Now it's time to go further back, back to a time when you and your husband or anyone else in your family might have lived together before. Go back to the time from which your current marital problems arise."

Martine immediately began to frown. Then she began to cry with little whimpering sobs.

"I'm so afraid. It's black, pitch black. I can't see anything. I'm just afraid. Something terrible is happening." Her voice was still childlike. I thought Martine was in some void, somewhere between lifetimes. But why was she afraid? I was confused.

"I'm going to tap you on the forehead and count backwards from three to one. When I say one, you'll see where you are."

It worked.

"I'm a young girl, sitting at a large wooden table in a big room. There isn't much furniture in the room, just the table really. I'm eating food from a bowl. It's like oatmeal. I have a big spoon."

"What's your name?"

"Rebecca," she answered. She did not know what year it was. But when Martine later died in this remembered lifetime, she stated that the year was 1859.

"Are you alone? Where are your parents?"

"I can't . . . I don't . . ." She began to cry again. "My father is there, but my mother is not. She's dead. I killed her!" Rebecca's mother, Martine went on to explain, had died during Rebecca's birth. Rebecca's father blamed his daughter for the death of his wife.

"He's awful to me. He beats me and locks me up all alone in the closet. I'm so scared!" she cried.

Now I understood why Martine had been so frightened to be in the dark void she had encountered earlier. It had not been a void after all. She had been a terrified little girl locked in a pitch-black closet. For how many hours had she been forced to suffer in darkness?

Rebecca's father, a woodcutter who worked with an axe, treated her like a slave. He gave her long lists of chores, constantly criticizing her, finding fault, beating her, and locking her in the dreaded closet. Martine tearfully recognized the man as Hal, her husband in her current life.

Rebecca never left her father. Despite his constant cruel and unloving behavior, she stayed with him until the end of his life.

I took her forward in time, to the day of his death. She was around thirty. After Rebecca's father died, I asked her what she felt.

"Relief . . . just immense relief. I'm so glad he's gone."

After her father's death, Rebecca married Tom, a man who treated her wonderfully. She recognized Tom as her current life son. Although Tom had wanted children, Rebecca did not, fearing that she would die in childbirth as her mother had. Nevertheless, they were very happy. Tom died first, then Rebecca. I progressed her in time to the last day of her life.

"I'm in bed. I'm an old lady with gray hair. I'm not frightened. I'm going to be with Tom." She died and floated over her body.

"What did you learn in that life?" I inquired.

"That I have to be assertive," she quickly responded. "I have to do what is right for me . . . when I am right . . . and not continue to suffer needlessly. I have to be assertive."

Emerging from the hypnotic state and remembering everything, Martine felt ecstatic. She felt stronger, relieved, and lighter, as if a heavy anchor around her neck had finally been removed.

"I've been repeating the same pattern," she observed, beaming brightly. "I don't have to do this any more!"

I noticed that Martine was actually shivering with the excitement of this discovery.

When she left the office, I did not know what would happen to Martine's marriage. But I knew that whatever happened, she would be dictating many more of the terms and conditions of their relationship. She would behave much more assertively and be much more in control.

She would be fine.

Two months later, Martine called me. She felt great, and her marriage had improved significantly since our regression session. She was "so much stronger." Perhaps in response to her new strength, Hal was being more considerate to her. Or perhaps some distant memory had reverberated inside him when she told him the details of her regression and his role in the recurrent pattern.

It is through relationships that we learn to express and receive love, to forgive, to help, and to serve.

From the experiences that some of my patients have in the "between life" state, I have come to believe that we actually pick our families for each lifetime before birth. We choose to live out the patterns that will afford us the most growth with the souls that will most effectively manifest these situations in our lives. Very often, these are souls we have met and interacted with in many ways in other lifetimes.

People always ask me whether they will be reunited with their loved ones in another life. I keep finding, and many other researchers concur, that we come around in groups, over and over again. We reincarnate with the same people. The group can become quite large, as the number of lifetimes increases, but the core group remains small and fairly constant. Relationships within the core group may change. For example, a mother-son relationship in one lifetime might recur as a sibling relationship in another, but the spirits or souls are the same. With regression experiences, recognition of the previous relationships can be brought to awareness.

The subconscious recognition of a person with whom we have had a past life connection is sometimes manifested by an immediate attraction or repulsion and by the repetition of the old behavior programming from the past life. The behavior may seem out of context or out of balance in the circumstances of the present life. This occurs most frequently in families or in couples where the relationships are closer and the bonds are more powerful. But past life recognition and acting out of ancient behavior patterns can also occur in many other relationships, such as boss-employee, neighbors, teacher and student, and even at the level of world leaders lunging at each other's throats.

Hope is a forty-five-year-old woman who discovered that she had once known a close family member in a completely different, nonfamilial context. Hope came to therapy complaining of a depression that seemed to be stimulated by the problems with her teenage son, Steve.

Steve was a poor student at a prestigious private school. He was also occasionally truant. Some of his problems stemmed from a learning disability. He also had a habit of speaking angrily to Hope, not listening to her, and testing her limits, which bothered his mother a great deal. Steve's problems did not seem inordinately severe to me. Hope appeared to be overreacting.

But Hope felt she had to protect herself from Steve. She felt he was depleting all of her energy, and that both her depression and Steve's problems were quickly becoming more acute. Hope had become convinced that life was nothing but one long struggle that would always leave her anxious and sad. She was also becoming convinced that she had to leave her son to protect herself, that he was cheating her out of her own life. The relationship was permeating every aspect of her day. As a result, Hope felt exhausted, almost as though she were seeping away. She was truly at the end of her rope.

However, as I interviewed Hope, it became clear to me that her feelings of struggle and hopelessness had not originated with her son. Her father had left the family when Hope was five. Hope's mother had died when the little girl was seven, orphaning both Hope and her younger brother. For two years Hope and her brother had been homeless. They cleaned and did chores for strangers in exchange for food and clothing, supplementing these meager earnings with what they found scavenging on the street.

When Hope was nine, her godmother finally found and rescued the children. But when Hope was thirteen, her godmother's family fell on financially difficult times, and they put Hope and her brother in state foster homes, where they lived for eighteen months. Eventually, Hope and her brother were able to return to the godmother's house where Hope stayed until she married at the age of twenty.

In the intervening years, Hope's marriage had endured four separations, but the family was still together. Things were looking up in many respects. At this point in life, Hope's family was doing much better financially.

When we tried to regress her to childhood, Hope had a great deal of trouble visualizing and letting go. She became so anxious about the possibility of reexperiencing childhood hurt that I decided it would be more constructive to bypass her childhood altogether.

At this suggestion, Hope was able to approach the regression process much more calmly. Soon she reported that she was a young man walking down a city street at the turn of the century. Hope entered a small apartment building where she found her employer in that lifetime. There she angrily and suddenly confronted the man, telling him she had realized that he had been taking advantage of the young man that she was, paying her almost nothing and advancing other employees at her expense.

Infuriated, Hope turned on her heel, walked out, and never came back again. This lifetime continued, but she never really found happiness because she carried this anger, this sense of being exploited by her employer, throughout the entire lifetime. Her perception and emotional reaction was that this had been a very intense and taboo betrayal, almost as though her employer had actually been her father.

But he was not her father. In fact, it was then that Hope realized that the man who had taken advantage of her so completely in that lifetime had reincarnated as her son, Steve.

After the regression, Hope seemed to see Steve more clearly. She realized that her relationship with him in this current lifetime is distinct from the one she had in the past lifetime. She recognized that she had been overreacting to his perceived transgressions. Steve was not a man intentionally trying to cheat her in business but a young person going through a perfectly natural, if trying, adolescent stage. If he had committed any transgressions against her at all in this lifetime, they were certainly petty.

Hope also realized that the themes of betrayal and being cheated are her issues, not Steve's. She understood that, in fact, they had cropped up very strongly in her childhood, many years before Steve was born. She recognized that not letting go of the anger she felt toward her employer in her past life hurt no one but herself, and that it was jeopardizing the joy she could feel from her relationship with Steve in this lifetime. We discussed the probability that her son's anger and acting out in this lifetime are related to her own behavior in the past life, when she turned on her heel and walked out on him.

Hope's therapy continues, and as it does she continues to gain more insight into which issues are hers to resolve, and becomes more aware that her anxiety and depression do not depend on her son. She has gotten more realistic and is gaining more perspective. I would not be surprised to find out that she and Steve have shared many other lifetimes together.

The parent-child relationship may be a very dramatic one, but its intensity and potential for growth do not, by any means, rule out the potential for humor, another great growth stimulator. I fondly remember the day when I was explaining to a workshop how we pick our family situations before birth in order to provide us with the greatest amount of growth possible. At this point, a mother in the group turned to her daughter, with whom she was clearly having a minor disagreement.

"See? *You're* the one who picked *me*," the woman told her teenager.

"Well, if I did, I must have been in a hurry!" the girl retorted without batting an eye.

This exchange, needless to say, was humorous, and the fact that this mother and daughter had chosen to attend the workshop together suggested that they actually had a very good relationship. Family members as well as couples can be regressed individually, as in any other past life exploration, or also simultaneously to resolve problems they share or to make a good relationship even more meaningful and insightful. Sometimes couples or members of the same family attend my workshops together. When they compare their regression experiences, they sometimes find that they have unknowingly regressed to the same lifetime and have found the others there. The improvement in relationships after such group regressions is often quite rapid and dramatic, similar to the improvement seen with individuals who get rid of chronic emotional or physical symptoms by regressing to the true precipitating causes of the problems, whether in this lifetime or another. In fact, some therapists who work with couples and families are already using regression therapy quite successfully in their practices. Adopted families are no different from biological children in this regard. I have regressed more than one adopted child who has discovered that he or she has shared previous lifetimes with his or her adoptive parents.

Patients do not always have to return to past lives to improve family relationships through hypnosis. Betsy was a patient who was having problems resolving her relationship with her authoritarian, strict, and distant father who was now deceased. The man had made her feel unloved. He had abused her emotionally by insulting her. He was so remote to Betsy that she had trouble dealing with him in therapy. Despite all of this, she still loved her father, but she couldn't take him off the pedestal long enough to see him accurately in order to deal with their relationship in an effective way.

In hypnosis I asked Betsy to visualize a very spiritual place in the form of a garden. In this garden her father came to her. He had just one message to her: "*Think of me as your brother.*"

And that did the trick. Once Betsy was able to think of her father as a brother, an equal, she was able to see both his virtues and his flaws much more clearly and comfortably. Then she was finally able to understand him, forgive him, and let him go.

The suggestion was so powerful that I have started to use it in therapy with other patients who have problems with one or both of their parents. In Freudian terms, it greatly eliminates the distortion caused by projection.

To share many lifetimes, joy and sorrow, achievement and despair, love and forgiveness, anger and grace, and, above all, endless growth with another soul is what it truly means to have a soulmate. A soulmate is often someone with whom we meet and feel an instant connection, as though we have known that person for a long time. In fact, we probably have. We do not have to be romantically involved with a person to experience the satisfaction and fulfillment of the soulmate connection.

Nor do we each have only one soulmate. The popular Western idea propagated by the philosopher Plato, that each of us has only one perfect other half who can "complete" our own incomplete soul, is only partially true. While others can seem to complete our experience—sharing and expanding our growth, intimacy, and joy—it is more likely that we have a soul group that consists of many soulmates. This may be a small group of souls that gets larger as we collect deep experiences with more and more souls over many lifetimes, but the feeling of having known a person before or sharing intense feelings and insights is certainly not limited to one person. We can even have more than one soulmate relationship at a time. Our romantic partner may complete our soul in one way, and so may, in other ways, a best friend, a parent, or a child.

As we grow by interacting with our soulmates, we ascend the ladder of lifetimes. We transcend old patterns, come to fully experience love and joy, and lose every last vestige of anger and fear. Eventually, we come to the point where we can voluntarily choose to be reborn to help others directly or even choose to stay in spirit form and help others from another level. Reincarnation for emotional growth is then no longer necessary. We can move from this path of growth to the path of growth through service.

To lose a soulmate to death or separation is by no means a loss of the opportunity to grow. A patient of mine recently lost her husband in an accident. She was absolutely devastated, certain that she had lost her soulmate and that nothing in life would ever have the same meaning or be worth anticipating. While her grief is very deep, real, and justified, we are working on the idea that she can look forward to future relationships that may be just as full of love, passion, intimacy, and growth.

A reunion with a soulmate after a long and involuntary separation can be an experience worth waiting for—even if the wait is one of centuries.

On a vacation in the Southwest, my former patient, Ariel, a biologist, met an Australian named Anthony. Both were emotionally mature individuals who had been married before, and they quickly fell in love and became engaged. Back in Miami, Ariel suggested that Anthony have a regression session with me just to see if he could have the experience and to "see what came up." They were both curious to find out whether Ariel would appear in any way in Anthony's regression.

Anthony turned out to be a superb regression subject. Almost instantly, he returned to a very vivid North African lifetime around the time of Hannibal, more than two thousand years ago. In that lifetime, Anthony had been a member of a very advanced civilization. His particular tribe was fair skinned, and they were gold smelters who had the ability to use liquid fire as a weapon by spreading it on the surface of rivers. Anthony was a young man in his mid-twenties in the midst of fighting a forty-day war with a neighboring, darker-skinned tribe that vastly outnumbered the defenders.

Anthony's tribe had actually trained some of the members of the enemy tribe in the art of warfare, and one of the former trainees was leading the assault. One hundred thousand of the enemy tribe carrying swords and hatchets were crossing a large river on ropes as Anthony and his people spread liquid fire on their own river, hoping it would reach the attackers before the attackers reached the shore.

To protect their women and children, the defending tribe put most of them on large boats with violet sails in the middle of a huge lake. Among this group was Anthony's young and beloved fiancée, who was perhaps seventeen or eighteen years old. However, the liquid fire suddenly burned out of control, and the boats caught fire. Most of the tribe's women and children perished in this tragic accident, including Anthony's fiancée, who was his great passion.

This tragedy broke the morale of the warriors, and they were soon defeated. Anthony was one of the few who escaped the slaughter through brutal hand-to-hand fighting. Eventually, he escaped to a secret passageway that led to a warren of rooms underneath the large temple where the tribe's treasures were stored.

There Anthony had found one other living person, his king. The king commanded Anthony to kill him, and Anthony, a loyal soldier, complied against his will. After the king's death, Anthony was all alone in the dark temple, where he used his time to write the history of his people on gold leaf and to seal the writings in large urns or jars. It was here that he eventually died of starvation and grief over the loss of his fiancée and his people.

There was one more detail. His fiancée in that lifetime reincarnated as Ariel in this lifetime. The two of them reunited as lovers after two thousand years. Finally, the long-postponed wedding would take place.

Anthony and Ariel had only been separated for one hour when he stepped out of my office. But the power of their reunion was such that it was as though they had not seen each other for two thousand years.

Recently Ariel and Anthony were married. Their sudden and intense and seemingly coincidental meeting now has a new layer of meaning to them, and their already passionate relationship is now infused with a sense of continuous adventure.

Anthony and Ariel plan to take a trip to North Africa to try and find the location of their past life together and to see what other details they can uncover. They know that whatever they find can only increase the adventure they find in each other.

6

Healing the Inner Child and the Abused Child

RECENTLY A GREAT DEAL OF ATTENTION HAS BEEN FOcused on "healing the inner child." John Bradshaw, among others, has helped popularize the technique of having a patient go back in time, in a relaxed and light hypnotic state, to discover the hurt, confused, and vulnerable child carried within as he or she grew up. This concept is one that evolved from psychoanalytic techniques. In the free associations made during traditional therapy, an intense emotional catharsis of traumatic childhood memories frequently occurs. As patients experience this process of remembering and emotional release, which clinicians call an abreaction, therapeutic changes and clinical improvement can occur.

Transactional analysis (TA) refined the psychoanalytic concept of recovering the repressed or forgotten painful memories from one's childhood. In *I'm OK, You're OK*, Dr. Eric Berne, the father of TA, stated that "every individual was once younger than he is now and that he carries within him fixated relics from earlier years which will be activated under certain circumstances. . . . Colloquially, everyone carries a little boy or girl around inside of him."

When childhood pain has not been resolved and emerges in the adult, it can produce a whole host of symptoms, including guilt, shame, depression, low self-esteem, and self-destructive behaviors. When people exhibit childish behavior, such as pouting, temper tantrums, and seeking excessive attention, the inner child is being triggered. If these triggering mechanisms are not brought to awareness, the maladaptive behavior that the patient suffered as a child can be turned against himself or herself and/or turned around and inflicted on others. Especially vulnerable are the patient's own children. For example, it is often found that an abusive parent was himself abused as a child. Freudian therapists label this "repetition compulsion." Bradshaw calls it "spontaneous age regression."

In TA theory, every person's psychological makeup contains three parts: the Child (the little boy or girl carried inside), the Adult (the rational objective part of the person now), and the Parent (the internalization of the parent or parent figure's thoughts, feelings, and actions). In TA therapy, actual dialogues between the Child, the Adult, and the Parent take place. The patient acts out the different roles.

A variation known as Psychodrama adds even more roles for tapping into our carried-over childhood fears and vulnerabilities during the therapeutic process. For example, an alter ego—a person observing words, behaviors, and body language—can comment as the various roles of Child, Adult, and Parent are enacted by others. Multiple participants, playing simultaneously, can shift roles, act out dramatic encounters, and experience the intense emotional release that occurs when painful childhood memories are brought into conscious awareness.

Bradshaw combined the concepts of TA with Erik Erikson's theory of personality development. In this way, he is able to pinpoint the problems and adapt his therapy to particular childhood stages.

The common thread in all of these techniques, as well as other methods employing dialogue with our "child," is the remembering and emotional release of painful childhood memories. In the inner child techniques, which are often effective and which are frequently used with adults who have grown up in dysfunctional, abusive, and alcoholic or drug-abusing families, contact with the memories of childhood is made while the person is in a relaxed state. Sometimes key words or phrases are used to focus in on the particular points in childhood from which the most painful memories arise. Sometimes the traumas are everywhere, in the day-in and day-out pounding of negative, undermining abuse from one's parents or significant others. Unlearning such negative programming is a vital part of therapy.

For example, in the relaxed state, the adult is sent back to find the "child" carried within his or her psyche for all these years. A childhood house is remembered and visualized, the rooms within, the family, and then the little child. The adult, with the increased perspective and understanding maturity has brought, talks to the child, reasons with the child, hugs the child, promises to protect the child, and brings the child out of the traumatic environment into the present time. In a sense, the child is rescued.

In theory, as the perspective of what happened to the child is broadened, the reactions to the childhood traumas are changed. This is called rescripting. It is as if the life-script is rewritten, the play altered. Hopefully, the inner child can now understand that he or she was not responsible for causing the parent's dysfunctional behavior and can now forgive the parent, or at least comprehend the reasons why the parent acted in such an irrational way. The adult becomes the loving parent of his or her own inner child.

Of course, the reality of past events has not changed at all. The only change occurs in the adult's internalized reactions to those events. He or she can let go of the pain, release the hurt, can heal the childhood wounds. The technique can be powerful. It can be the first step toward a cure.

But sometimes even these emotional and moving childhood abreactions are not enough. Sometimes there is more than one childhood involved. Sometimes the roots of the pain go even further back.

Linda is an attractive thirty-five-year-old attorney from a small town in central Pennsylvania. She is divorced from a psychologically abusive husband. Linda came to my office well dressed in a navy-blue suit and an open-necked blouse. She wore no jewelry except for a large diamond ring. Linda seemed cool and controlled and effortlessly projected the image of a successful female professional.

As our first session got underway and Linda recounted her history, I was surprised by the violence of her childhood, by the volcanic rumblings under that cool exterior. Linda had no memories of her life before she was eight years old. She could not even picture what her parents looked like when she was young. But she did remember how her father had beaten her with belts, fists, coat hangers, and wooden beams. He had frequently choked her, calling her "whore, sleaze, bitch," when she was just a young girl. Linda's mother told her that the beatings had started at a very early age. At times, her mother had joined in, beating her daughter and scratching her with her fingernails. Linda had also been repeatedly sexually molested by an uncle, with her parents' knowledge.

As I began to comprehend the level of abuse this young child had endured, I started to feel a twinge of nausea. Even as a child, Linda had been so responsible that she had assumed the role of a surrogate mother to her younger siblings and had tried to protect them from being treated in the same way. As a result, she had suffered the brunt of her parents' abuse. Linda had even called the Child Welfare Department several times in order to get the state to intervene and protect the younger children, to no avail. Her parents denied all the allegations. Then, when the investigating social worker left, Linda's father beat her nearly to the point of unconsciousness.

During her teenage years, Linda had developed asthma. She also had a chronic, severe fear of choking. She could not tolerate wearing anything around her neck—not jewelry, not a scarf, not even a sweater. The necklines of her clothes were stretched from her pulling on them. She could never button the top button of any blouse she was wearing.

Linda had tried to run away from home several times, but there was no place to go. Finally, she went away to college and married at a young age to ensure that she would never have to go home again.

During that first session, I began to try to unravel the threads of Linda's tortured history, but Linda could remember nothing before the fourth grade. I wasn't surprised. Such a memory loss can be a merciful thing, especially when the past has been so violent and abusive. But Linda was unhappy, frightened, and beset by a myriad of symptoms such as recurring nightmares, phobias, and sudden panic attacks, as well as an overwhelming dread of choking and of having anyone or anything touch her neck.

I knew we would have to explore her past.

I gave her an audiotape to take home. On the front side of this tape is a relaxation meditation, and on the back is a regression exercise. My voice guides both of the audio journeys. I told Linda that she was free to listen to either or both sides and to call me if the tape induced too much anxiety or negative emotion.

At home, she listened to the tape, playing both sides daily. The tape made her feel very relaxed. In fact, every time she listened she fell asleep. However, her symptoms and her paralyzing fears persisted unchanged.

Linda came in for her second session eager to try hypnosis. She quickly reached a moderately deep level of trance state. I guided her back to her childhood, and Linda could now remember more details of the fourth grade, such as her classroom and her kindly teacher. Now she could finally picture her father's face as he appeared when she was eight. She began to sob. I worked with the "inner child," instructing Linda to send her adult self back to hug, talk to, comfort, and rescue the vulnerable eight-year-old. She was filled with fear, relief, and gratitude, and she was comforted. She attempted to understand and to forgive her father.

I then used techniques I had developed over the years to help her release the fears, to see things from the adult's perspective. I used the methods of John Bradshaw and others who have worked with the vulnerable, frightened inner child. We talked, reasoned, felt, projected light and love, reviewed, cried, analyzed, synthesized, and rescripted. For ninety minutes, the cleansing of Linda's childhood continued. When she finally emerged from the hypnotic state, Linda felt somewhat better.

Linda started to sing again, something she enjoyed but had not been able to do since childhood, when she had sung in the church choir. Her memory was somewhat better. She felt less anxious, and her mood was improved. But Linda's life was still filled with fears. She remained terrified of choking, and she still could not tolerate having anything near her neck. Her asthma persisted. We had more work to do.

At her third session, I used a rapid induction technique that produces a deep level of hypnosis within thirty seconds. Linda was immediately racked with sobs and began to arch her neck.

"Someone is grabbing my hair and pulling my head back!" she screamed. "They are going to guillotine me!"

She had gone directly to a death experience. I assumed Linda was in France, but she corrected me. She was in England. (This confused me, as I had assumed that guillotining only happened in France. That evening, I researched the topic and found out that for a brief time guillotining was also practiced in England, Scotland, and various other European countries.)

From the trance state, Linda watched herself being decapitated. She told me that she had a five-year-old daughter in that lifetime and that this child was in the crowd, also watching. After the beheading, Linda's head was put into a burlap sack and thrown into the nearby river. We went through the death scene several times, lessening the emotion each time, until she could calmly tell me everything that had happened. Her heart was broken because she had to leave her young daughter.

A few moments passed. I could see her eyelids fluttering and her eyes moving under her closed lids as she seemed to be scanning something. Suddenly she was sobbing again, thrashing her head from side to side.

"It's him! It's my father!" I knew Linda meant her father in her current life, a fact she confirmed to me after the regression was over. "He was my husband. He arranged my execution so that he could be with another woman. He had me killed!"

Now Linda understood why her mother had told her that Linda had seemed to hate her father from the moment she was born. She would cry and scream when he picked her up. She would stop when he put her down. Now it made sense to her.

Linda remembered two other past lives during this session.

Several centuries ago, she had been an Italian woman who was happily married to her present life grandfather. She could vividly see herself in the boat the couple had owned. She was wearing a white dress, and her long, dark hair billowed in the breeze. This life had been a happy one filled with love, and she had died peacefully at an old age. In her current lifetime, Linda has a very warm and loving relationship with her grandfather.

In a glimpse of a third lifetime, she saw herself on a large farm with haystacks and a windmill. She was an old lady with a large family.

I asked Linda what she needed to learn from these lifetimes.

"Not to hate," she quickly answered from the higher perspective of her superconscious mind. "I must learn to forgive and not to hate."

The energy of her hate and that of her father's violent anger was what had drawn them together again in this lifetime, and the consequences had been disastrous. But now she remembered. Now the healing could begin. Linda could understand why she had immediately rejected her father and why he, tapping a wellspring of guilt, shame, and violence, had repeatedly erupted into a torrent of abusiveness. Now she could begin to forgive.

When the regression was over, I asked Linda to button the top button of her blouse. She did so without hesitation and without a hint of anxiety or fear.

She was cured.

The cure had taken three sessions. Her symptoms have not recurred. Even her asthma is nearly gone.

The intensive second session in which we worked with and rescued Linda's inner child was important, and it did help her. But the regression to the guillotine lifetime proved to be the curative factor.

In cases like Linda's, inner child work and the ensuing catharsis act as a doorway to healing that is best and most effectively accomplished through past life therapy. Traumas experienced in this lifetime's childhood are sometimes variations on traumas experienced in other lifetimes. These prior lifetimes may be the true source of this childhood's pain. Reexperiencing the source of the problem can heal the current lifetime's inner child.

Laura, a twenty-five-year-old manager of a boutique, came in with many symptoms. Laura suffered from intermittent depression and had a long history of eating disorders for which she regularly attended support and therapy groups like Overeaters Anonymous. But perhaps Laura's most troubling symptom was the question in her mind about whether or not she had been sexually abused as a child. Laura had no clear or even partial memories of such an experience. It was more a feeling or a pattern of kinesthetic impressions she would sometimes have about an older person touching her.

As I took Laura's introductory history, she related that her parents were estranged and that her relationship with them was distant. There were long periods of time in which she didn't speak to them at all, and when she did speak to them, both she and they would become overwhelmed with so much anxiety and discomfort that she felt like she was "drowning." We also uncovered what was perhaps a more significant detail of her past. When Laura tried to remember anything about her childhood, she drew a blank. She had no memories of childhood at all.

We decided to approach this symptom initially. But first we reviewed the past life memories Laura had experienced when she had attended a seminar of mine a few months earlier that had prompted her to decide to explore her problems further in individual therapy.

During the group regression, Laura had recalled having been a thirteen-year-old French boy carrying a bow and arrow. She was shot in the chest by someone else's arrow and died. Laura recognized that her grandmother in that lifetime was her mother in this lifetime. In another lifetime, Laura had been a London street person and pickpocket. And, in a third, she had been a fifteen-year-old girl living in Spain in the sixteenth century.

As Laura entered that Spanish lifetime, she was being tied to a stake to be burned as a witch because she had healed a boy in her village. Laura recognized that the judge who had pronounced her death sentence in that lifetime is her father in this lifetime. These memories had not scared Laura. Thinking that she might be eternal made Laura feel very free and happy. It also made her feel there was hope for her problems, and her depression had lifted somewhat.

The next time Laura came in she could again access no memories from childhood, but she still wanted to uncover the root of her problem. Because Laura was so successful with past life regression in the seminar, we decided that this was the easiest route for her therapy and that we should approach her problems with regression again.

Once more, Laura accessed memories of dying at a young age. This time she was a fourteen-year-old boy in fifteenth-century France and a member of a well-to-do family. Her parents owned an apple orchard. Tragically, a fatal epidemic overtook the community and the mode of transmission involved Laura's family's apples. However, the family members were completely unaware of the danger their crop posed, and they were not at fault. Laura had died in this epidemic, but not before she recognized that her parents in this lifetime had been her parents in that lifetime.

As we reviewed the lifetime after her emergence from hypnosis, issues of anger, love, and forgiveness came up. Laura had to forgive her parents in that lifetime because they hadn't purposely poisoned her. She needed to release that anger.

At home, Laura had used my relaxation and regression tape to explore the answers to the question of what had happened to her during her childhood. The intuitive answers she obtained were often spiritual in nature, advising her that the experience concerned learning about balance, moderation, and harmony. By experiencing the unbalanced, immoderate lifetimes, she had become patient and loving. And, her intuitive mind told her, these experiences were really the foundation of true wisdom.

After this regression, it was as if a logjam had been somehow loosened. Laura's childhood memories from her current lifetime began to surface, and when they did, it was clear why the memories had been blocked. Laura's fleeting impressions of abuse had been accurate. Laura had indeed been sexually abused by her father and her uncle. From the time she was two, they had fondled and touched her, and had forced her to perform oral sex. This abuse had continued for years. Worst of all, Laura remembered that her mother had been aware of this abuse, but she had done nothing to stop it.

These memories, particularly the memory of her mother's complicity, heightened Laura's symptoms and problems for a brief time. Over time, she had the opportunity to integrate these experiences and feelings in therapy. As she did so, Laura began to release the anger about these memories, and her eating disorder started to improve rapidly.

Laura was also able to put her father's and her uncle's abusive behavior into perspective. She was able to see that the history of her father tormenting her goes way back. Although he did not specifically abuse her in that past lifetime, he did have her executed. Therefore, this man's perception of the usual boundaries between parents and children may have been blurred in this lifetime. His sexual impulses toward her may have been stronger than if there had been no past life connection between the two. She was also able to see that she had been in a series of lifetimes in which parental figures had not been able to protect her from death or poverty, and that this series of lifetimes had provided lessons in love and patience and wisdom.

Laura's past life connection with her father is typical in present life abusive relationships. Often, a past life history in which the current abuser has somehow jeopardized or harmed the current victim makes it more likely that an abuser will transgress boundaries and incest taboos in the present lifetime. It is as if the essential boundaries and limits that maintain safety and well-being between the two are already weakened; they have already been crossed. This seems to make it harder for both participants to avoid falling into a new variation on that long-standing pattern of abuse, pain, and abandonment. This does not mean that victims of abuse deserve or ask for abuse or that they are destined to repeat this pattern lifetime after lifetime. There is always free will. Such a volatile situation can create very special conditions for accelerated emotional and spiritual growth. Temptations can be overcome and lessons learned.

It is significant that Laura had not been able to access any real childhood memories until the past life context was established. Only after Laura had gained that larger perspective could the memory of her current, painful childhood be released to the surface. Only then could the inner child be comforted. A catharsis could take place. The healing could begin.

It was almost an anticlimax when we discovered that Laura's eating disorder was alleviated. Today, her weight is still slowly dropping, and she is no longer on a cycle of binging. Her depression has lifted. She meets occasionally with her parents to try and resolve their relationship, and her anxiety about these meetings has lessened greatly. After many years of struggling with her symptoms and trying to understand them through other forms of therapy, Laura found a rapid and lasting cure.

The incidence of abuse against children in this country is startlingly high. Approximately one in three girls is a childhood victim of sexual abuse, and one out of five boys is victimized sexually. Past life therapy can be important to the healing process because for many adult survivors it provides a rapid, safe way of unlocking and clearing the experience, and because it also offers a larger emotional and spiritual framework in which to process and integrate the memories and feelings that are released during the healing process. Past life therapy gives victims new handles and hooks for approaching and grasping their experiences.

In the hands of a trained therapist, past life therapy for sexual abuse is not dangerous. In the therapeutic situation, no victim needs to be afraid of reexperiencing painful, repressed memories. In my experience with patients like Laura, reexperiencing memories in this context is characterized by a feeling of liberation. Therapy enables the victim to comfort this lifetime's inner child. Many aspects of adult life, particularly relationships, are improved.

A blocked memory of sexual abuse presents a monumental challenge to our ability to find joy, satisfaction, and intimacy in adult relationships. The tendency is for adult survivors of abuse to shy away from intimacy in their relationships in a symbolic bid to protect themselves from reexperiencing the buried pain. This tendency is another manifestation of the same dynamic that prompts women to symbolically protect themselves from hurt with a sexual origin by becoming overweight to mask physical attractiveness. We will discuss this aspect further in the next chapter.

Dr. John Briere, a researcher in the Department of Psychiatry at the University of Southern California School of Medicine, said that one of the most painful insights he has repeatedly heard from adult victims of childhood sexual abuse is "knowing Daddy hurt me for his benefit. Daddy was willing to sacrifice my needs for his needs." Dr. Briere also observed that a victim of child abuse ". . . loses that notion that you can depend on a warm, caring caretaker; a sense that you often never get back." Instead, that reality is replaced with one in which a child knows that a "seemingly 'good' person is quite capable of being 'bad.' " That sense of trust is shattered.

Dr. David L. Corwin, a professor of psychiatry at the Washington University School of Medicine, has observed that a profound sense of deprivation and of seriously impaired self-esteem frequently results from childhood molestation by the father. The result is that "those affects and attitudes undermine a person's ability to stand up and protect herself, to feel that she has the right as a person to expect and demand that she be treated in a respectful, caring, appropriate manner." The women "begin to think of themselves as bad to preserve the image of an idealized . . . father." Therapy can then "help the childhood abuse victim 'unlearn' negative self-concepts and become a survivor in the fullest sense."

The abuse need not occur in the present lifetime or in childhood in order to influence the present lifetime's relationships.

Emily was a forty-three-year-old woman who came into the office suffering from what she described as "unrealistic fears." She had anxiety and panic attacks, fear of abandonment and loss, and an aversion to sex, particularly to ejaculation. As a result, her relationship with her husband was very troubled. She was afraid of this man with whom she had shared so much of her life. Needless to say, many conflicts in the relationship had resulted from these feelings. Emily's high-school-aged son had recently died in an automobile accident, and she was still grieving. Emily was also a member of Alcoholics Anonymous, where she was doing well with no relapses.

In past life therapy Emily returned to a time when she was a dark-haired woman wearing a red dress, dancing dreamily with a young man at a party. This young man was Emily's dead son.

In the second key memory of this session, Emily recalled having been a destitute young mother in the time of King Herod. The ruler's command to kill all children two years old and under had just been issued, and Emily had accidentally smothered her own son in an attempt to hide the crying child from the king's soldiers.

In the Middle Ages Emily had another lifetime with her lost son. This time she had been his sister, and the two had shared a very close relationship. The brother had been slain by sword while he was riding on horseback in the midst of a battle. Both she and her father had been devastated by the boy's death. The father never recovered from the loss. Emily married a rich man to escape her father and their shared sadness. The husband had subjected her to rough, crude, and unpleasant lovemaking with no sensitivity to her pleasure or comfort. This physical relationship had terrified Emily. It had also resulted in the birth of three children.

In a subsequent session, Emily recalled having been a French gypsy and peasant woman in the mid-nineteenth century. She had several children who depended on her, and she had to resort to prostitution to feed them. Emily was despised for her trade, and although she cared for some of the men, she was violently abused by others. In a particularly harrowing incident, some of them even spat at her during the abuse and degradation.

As she grew older in that lifetime and her children no longer depended on her for their survival, Emily turned to alcohol, and she eventually committed suicide.

After this second session, Emily was able to make many connections to her present life issues. Realizing that she had known her son many times before, Emily was able to resolve the lingering grief over his death.

One very strong theme for her was her love of children. Emily works in the pediatric ward of a hospital and volunteers with children.

Another theme was sexual abuse and cruelty. Emily was able to understand the past life roots of her present life aversion to sexual contact. She could see that in this particular constellation of lifetimes, sex had been primarily a vehicle for degradation and pain. She also made a connection between her aversion to ejaculation and the humiliating spitting she had endured in nineteenth-century France. Emily was able to shed some of her fear of sex. She understood that the fear was a protection against pain that she did not have to endure in this lifetime, that this pain belonged in the past.

With understanding came the beginning of healing. Emily had been in traditional psychoanalysis for years, with no improvement of her symptoms. This was not the fault of her analyst, but rather had more to do with the scope of the material covered. The roots of Emily's problems simply lay beyond her present life experiences. It was necessary to address past life memories and traumas in order to effect a cure. In this sense, past life therapy for abuse is merely an expansion of psychoanalytic thought and treatment into a larger arena.

Today, Emily's sexual fears are diminishing. As a result, her relationship with her husband has become less charged. It is still not a perfect relationship. However, it has important strengths, and Emily is able to evaluate its pros and cons from a more realistic perspective. She is also no longer afraid of having a future relationship with another man, should she eventually decide to make that choice.

The shadows of the past have lifted. Her fears of sexual contact and of men have been fading away. Whatever choice Emily makes about her marital relationship, it will be clear-sighted and realistic as a result of her past life memories, and not the result of a projection of her own fears onto the marriage.

Once the memories are accessed, the healing process begins. Some typical patterns of healing from sexual abuse are documented in the excellent book *The Courage to Heal* by Ellen Bass and Linda Davis. The first step in that process is the decision to heal, to seek help.

Like Laura, victims often have partial or shadow memories of their abuse as those memories first start to surface. Often, as in Emily's case, there is a symptomatic inability to form intimate relationships. And, as all of the cases indicate, there is a high level of discomfort.

As we have seen, frequently the memory of abuse becomes more easily accessible during regression therapy. Victims can begin to become aware that the frightening elements of their dreams and daydreams and the tips of those elusive memory fragments are really all connected to the overriding childhood trauma.

A subsequent stage in the healing process is the ability to accept that the memories of the abuse are real. Doing so is a vital part of the healing process. Hypnotic regression to this childhood and to other lifetimes is a technique that is ideally suited to accepting such memories. Patients see and feel their experiences vividly, yet they feel safe and are able to integrate their memories afterwards in the protected therapeutic situation. The patient knows that these are memories, not fantasies, due to the intensity of the memories and emotions accessed through regression, and the experience of this intensity counteracts the mental defense mechanism of denial. Dr. Wayne Dyer, author of *Your Erroneous Zones*, reminds us that mental acceptance often lags behind emotional when he says that "You'll see it when you believe it." But for many patients seeing *is* still believing. And seeing the past with hypnotic regression does allow some otherwise denial-prone patients to accept their pasts more effortlessly, thus speeding the healing process.

Survivors of abuse often pass through another stage of healing—that of feeling shame about their experiences, shame for participating in an activity that is taboo. But patients who access these memories through hypnotic regression are able to integrate more easily the fact that as small children they were never responsible for the adult's behavior. Past life memory also helps dissipate shame as it helps explain why boundaries that should have been impermeable in these formative relationships with significant adults were broken.

This brings us to the highly charged subject of anger. Survivors are typically encouraged to experience their anger toward their abuser, to feel that this anger is healing. While anger is certainly a stage that must be traversed, I have found that when past life therapy is employed, anger is often rather quickly transmuted into understanding. In my practice, this stage is often comparatively short.

I am not exactly sure why this happens, and more research certainly needs to be done. It may be that the greater perspective that is afforded by past life experience allows the victim to become more dispassionate more quickly. Or, perhaps, the spiritual component of the therapy can, in some cases, provide a quicker growth and healing curve.

Ever since Dr. Elisabeth Kübler-Ross delineated the stages of grief, it has often been assumed that one must go thoroughly and methodically through every stage of every process for complete healing to take place. But not every individual who is undergoing a healing process needs to go through every stage in a rigid time sequence. It is not essential, for example, that anger be expressed for a protracted period even though your therapist may think it is necessary. After reexperiencing the visual and empathic review in past life therapy, understanding sometimes quickly follows. This type of therapy does seem to have a special facility for short-circuiting the anger phase.

It encourages a patient to work at his or her own pace, whatever that pace may be. Why experience anger for months when you can rid yourself of it in an hour, a day, or a week? As Laura's and Linda's cases demonstrate, through the understanding that past life therapy provides, anger can be diminished and the trauma can be more quickly resolved.

This is not a promise of a "quick fix," nor a "scolding" for patients and therapists who proceed at a slower and, in their cases, more appropriate rate. It simply highlights another choice a survivor can make.

Once you understand the roots of your anger, you can choose to release it whenever you want. You can keep it, if you feel more comfortable about that, but you can also let anger go at any time. The choice is yours. Everyone has his or her own unique and perfect pace of healing and growth.

A patient who unlocks memories of abuse in this lifetime and perhaps other lifetimes through hypnotic regression does not forget the memory of the anger. But such a patient seems to be much quicker to forgive himself or herself and others. A deep level of forgiveness often seems to be the spiritual lesson of abuse experiences.

Lorraine knew forgiveness was part of her lesson even before she came to therapy. As she sat in my office, this thirty-seven-year-old college professor and administrator recounted how unnurturing her parents had been to her when she was a young child. Her mother had suffered from a severe case of rheumatoid arthritis, and this illness demanded all of her parents' attention. Lorraine felt that her mother and father had both been cold and unaffectionate toward her. To make matters worse, Lorraine's father had died of a heart attack when she was six years old.

Lorraine felt that her relationship with her parents and her father's death had made it very difficult for her to be intimate with other people, and also to be forgiving of herself and others. She was afraid that if she got close to people that she would either lose them or become very angry with them. Lorraine had been a DES baby, and her fears of infertility played into this fear of intimacy.

In past life therapy, Lorraine recalled a lifetime in ancient Greece. In that lifetime, her present father had been her father once again, and in that past lifetime he had abused her sexually in her early childhood. Eventually, he had been discovered and taken away. Lorraine thought he had probably been killed by the authorities for what he had done. Significantly, in this lifetime Lorraine's father had also left her life in her sixth year.

Mixed in with her anger, Lorraine also felt a great deal of guilt that she had been the cause of her father's punishment in the Greek lifetime. She realized that in this present lifetime she felt not only angry toward her father but guilty about feeling angry, that the pattern of abuse was in fact an old one, and that she had to forgive herself and him in order to let go of the anger. It was also clear that Lorraine's inability to forgive in other relationships was also tied up with being abused by her father in her past lifetime.

Lorraine also recognized that she had to forgive her father "twice" for leaving her at such a young age. She is working on that now and is feeling much better about her relationship with him in this lifetime. Her feelings of both abandonment and anger are abating. She has come to realize that experiencing a fatal heart attack is not the same as being taken away for committing abuse. She is able to see her father's life pattern more clearly, to see that many of the events in this lifetime of his had played out in a kind of karmic counterpoint to the lifetime in which he had abused her. She believes that, in a way, he was forced to leave her again when she was six as a kind of repayment for the abuse he had committed in the other lifetime and that, in fact, he had not wanted to leave her at all. She has also seen that the character of her father in this lifetime was a vast improvement over his in the Greek lifetime. This, too, was healing. Lorraine has become very sympathetic and compassionate about her father's difficult path of growth.

Lorraine's ability to be understanding and feel forgiveness resulted quickly, largely from her being able to see her father's flow of lifetimes. Simply perceiving an overall purpose or logic to events that have been painful can be enough to heal by releasing anger and replacing it with forgiveness. This process is not necessarily logical, but I have seen it take place many times.

Lorraine is also now much less fearful of intimacy than before, because she now knows that her father's abandonment and abuse took place in a very specific situation. It was not due to a defect or impairment in her. Therefore, she has no reason to believe that others will also leave her.

Like so many cases, Mercedes, a forty-year-old single woman, came into the office complaining of stress, anxiety, nightmares, and headaches. A successful businesswoman, Mercedes had been educated in parochial schools. Mercedes was spiritually aware in many areas, and had meditated for many years. One odd symptom that she recounted to me occurred when she meditated. During meditation, she would experience a sudden involuntary turning of her head to one side, as if protecting herself from something.

For many sessions we tried traditional therapy methods; there was only a slight improvement in her symptoms. Finally, Mercedes decided to try regression therapy. The therapy, which at first was directed to this lifetime's childhood, brought out quite a bit of hurt as Mercedes began to recall being molested by her drunken and surly father, a man who had died ten years ago. In this session, she found herself turning away and gagging from the oral sex that had been forced upon her by her father. Here was the cause of the head turning that took place during Mercedes's meditations.

Mercedes also remembered her shame and confusion, becoming somewhat upset and depressed when her father ended his abuse and went back to her mother. Unfortunately, the abuse was the only affection or attention this child ever received. When Mercedes recalled the childhood emotions attached to the abuse, fear was not the first one on the list. Disgust was the more salient emotion, as if she were already quite used to this experience. Apparently, the abuse had been ongoing for some time.

In subsequent sessions Mercedes uncovered memories of physical abuse from her mother. Her mother had beaten her frequently, impulsively, and without warning, frightening the child terribly. She now understood why she doesn't trust women.

She uncovered a memory of her father fondling her at the age of one while she was in her bassinet, a very early memory. But Mercedes also recalled how much she loved her father and how much he loved her, even though he abused her. This was extremely confusing to Mercedes.

In her next session Mercedes regressed to a past life. She had been a twenty-six-year-old woman who lived in the Dark Ages. She remembered being a slave who was chained to the wall of the castle kitchen where she had constantly labored. In this lifetime, Mercedes had only been removed from her chains for one purpose—to be taken to a locked room in the castle to meet a man who used her sexually. Mercedes recalled feeling more disgust than any other emotion after these encounters, a disgust that was not dissimilar to her feeling of being abused by the father who loved her.

Mercedes felt immediate relief after this session. She had

achieved much more understanding about her sexual attitudes and biases. Like other survivors of abuse, intimacy was an overwhelming challenge for Mercedes. Mercedes enjoyed sex, but for her sexual contact was shielding and mechanical, not at all intimate. After this regression, she felt happier and more hopeful. She is now beginning to understand and resolve her past and her present, to look forward to the future.

One of the most interesting points about Mercedes's case is the experience of her siblings. She had two sisters, but only one of them had been abused by her father. The other, who was the middle sister, was always left alone.

One possible explanation for this is that the untouched child did not have a history of abuse or taboo transgression with the father in a previous lifetime. Their connection, if any, may have taken place in a different sphere, a different constellation of behaviors, lessons, and circumstances.

People often bring up the idea of "karma": that as far as lifetime experiences and circumstances go, what we sow in one lifetime is what we reap in the next. This is not always strictly true. I believe that experiences like these are not necessarily punishments from the past, or even lessons or patterns carried forward from past lives. By choosing to come into a particular family or constellation of circumstances you have not agreed to submit to abuse. However, you have agreed to participate in a certain lesson or type of drama. You still have free will about how a particular lesson or teaching is carried out and so do the other individuals who have chosen to share the lifetime with you. Just because you have agreed to play a role in this family, abuse is not the invariable result. Part of the learning process is learning *not* to choose the more harmful or destructive paths. Growth can occur easily and joyfully as well as through struggle, and there are many gradations between the two.

The potential for abuse will exist, but it is not inevitable. In this sense, all families are like little interactive worlds or universes, small emotional and spiritual ecosystems that constantly interact, readjust, and interact yet again. This is one way to understand why abuse occurs between certain family members and not others.

Past life therapy fosters greater awareness of larger issues and more complex and expansive situations. When the shadows are there and memories aren't clear, there is nothing tangible to grieve about or to release. But when appropriate memories are recalled, an abusive victim has a place to "push off from" into future growth.

When we understand reasons, patterns, and causes, we experience what many call grace. The grace of understanding allows us to transcend the traditional idea of karma, so that we do not have to reenact the same old dramas. We absolve ourselves of the need to repeat them, the need to experience pain. We enter a higher flow where the keynote of our lifetimes can become one of harmony and joy.

Finally, victims of abuse need to remember that even in these challenging circumstances, the soul is never harmed. The spirit is indestructible and immortal.

7

Healing the Need to Protect: Uncovering the Sources of Obesity and Substance Abuse

KATHY IS A THIRTY-EIGHT-YEAR-OLD BUSINESS EXECUTIVE who came to me for the treatment of her anxiety symptoms. Kathy suffered from a severe and escalating fear of driving a car, which was manifested by panic attacks on expressways. Sometimes Kathy would even panic in cars when she was travelling as a passenger.

During these attacks, Kathy would experience sweating, palpitations, a racing heartbeat, difficulty catching her breath, and shakiness. Her vision would become "blurry." By the time she came to see me, Kathy had become so terrified of losing control of the wheel that she had to take a tranquilizer before driving on a highway.

Kathy had tried psychotherapy and biofeedback, but neither type of therapy had been able to eradicate her symptoms. Neurological evaluations had been normal. Kathy did not suffer from the form of heart disease called mitral valve prolapse, which is often associated with anxiety attacks. When I took Kathy's psychological history during our first session, I discovered that nothing about her past was particularly traumatic or abusive. Her physical health was good, except for the fact that Kathy was forty pounds overweight.

During our second session, I decided to try hypnosis. Kathy quickly relaxed into a deep hypnotic state, and I could see her eyes scanning under her closed and fluttering eyelids. Before I could even direct her to go back in time to the origin of her driving phobia, Kathy began to tell me about a couple of long-forgotten, but very traumatizing, automobile accidents from early childhood. The first car she had been travelling in hit a patch of ice and swerved out of control. Kathy had been terrified by the resulting crash and the injuries that members of her family had suffered, although she herself had not been injured. In the second accident, the brakes had failed as the car went down a hill. Everyone in the car had almost been killed. Kathy cried as she remembered these dreadful episodes, but after these long-forgotten traumas had seeped back into her awareness, the driving phobia gradually disappeared. Her confidence increased, and she no longer feared losing control of the wheel. The panic attacks subsided.

Flushed with success and feeling wonderful, Kathy soon scheduled a third session to see if we could do something about her weight. Kathy stated that she had been obese "as long as I can remember." Dieting would help for a while, but then she would rapidly regain all of the weight she had lost.

On the large reclining chair in my office, Kathy drifted into the familiar trance state. Soon she entered a past life. She reported that she saw herself as "a very bony woman, skinny and out of proportion, like a skeleton with skin. There are men in uniforms there . . . I have acid burns on my body! They are doing medical experiments—torture—on me!"

Kathy cried as she saw herself as a victim of the inhumane Nazi medical experiments conducted in the concentration camps of World War II. She died in one of these camps, by then a helpless skeleton finally being freed from its pain. She floated above her body and soon found a brilliant light to which she was magnetically drawn. The light comforted her, and Kathy experienced a feeling of incredible peace and love.

The session was not over, however. Kathy's eyes were fluttering again.

"I am in a French-looking place. It is New Orleans. I have had many men because I am a prostitute." In that lifetime, Kathy had contracted a chronic, debilitating sexually transmitted disease, and she was dying. She was wasting away, starving because of the illness. Once again, her body was like a living skeleton. Kathy died in the same bed in which she had contracted her lethal disease. Once again, Kathy floated above her body. And, once again, she found the brilliant light that did not hurt her eyes.

"I never found someone to love in that life," she wistfully observed. Her spirit had starved as had her body.

In both of these past life memories, she had died in a state of starvation. She was literally just skin and bones.

"Is there a connection between these two lifetimes and your current weight problem?" I asked, remembering the original intent of this session.

The answer came quickly and effortlessly. "In this life, I needed the extra weight for protection. I needed to guarantee that I would not starve again." After a pause Kathy added, "But now I no longer need this protection."

Because Kathy had remembered the traumas of starvation, she no longer needed layers of fat to protect her.

Over the next six or eight months, Kathy slowly and steadily lost all of her extra weight. At the time of this writing, she has sustained the loss. Perhaps even more significantly, Kathy has started a wonderful new romantic relationship since losing the weight. Feeling good about herself and liking how she looks definitely played an important part in Kathy's ability to let this new relationship into her life.

When Dee, a banker's wife, came to see me, her primary symptom was obesity. Dee was fifty to sixty pounds overweight, and she had been trying to lose that weight for years. Dee had tried everything—special diets, hypnosis, psychotherapy, medications, fasting, spas, and exercise regimens. But nothing had worked. Dee was a classic "yo-yo" dieter. She would get down to a certain weight, become anxious, and then quickly regain all the lost pounds.

All told, Dee had lost and gained hundreds of pounds over the years.

Dee is a very striking woman, and one therapist she had consulted suspected that Dee was afraid that men would be attracted to her if she were thin. However, exhaustive therapy in this area proved as futile as everything else.

In my office, Dee slipped into a trance and saw herself two or three hundred years ago as a young Native American woman who had been "stolen" by a male from another tribe. He had singled her out for her great beauty. She had been kidnaped, raped, and mutilated by this man. Dee had spent the rest of that lifetime in suffering and agony. Although the experience had not killed her, the pain she had endured made her resolve never to be beautiful again.

Instead, the Native American woman became fat. That obesity persisted even into the current lifetime.

Dee's earlier therapist had been correct. Dee was indeed afraid of becoming thin and of then having strangers become sexually attracted to her. Dee had not entered a sexual relationship with her husband until their courtship was well underway and a feeling of familiarity and safety had been well established. But since the root cause of Dee's problem had not originated in her current lifetime, the therapy had failed.

In one hypnotherapy session Dee had remembered, and she was cured. The pounds dropped off quickly, and she passed below her previous threshold weight. Dee kept losing until she decided to level off. As she lost the weight, she did not reexperience any anxiety, fear, or reflexive binge eating. And, as a bonus, she no longer feared death. Not only had she become thin, she had also realized that she was immortal. One session!

Dee has now maintained her ideal weight for almost four years. Her regression experience has also stimulated an interest in spiritual matters, and this aspect of life is now a very important and rewarding one to her.

Dee and Kathy are only two of a group of patients, mostly women, who have successfully conquered chronic obesity with the help of past life regression. In my experience, the need to protect the physical body from a previous experience of pain, starvation, sexual abuse, or violence is a cause of obesity that often originates in past lives and that can thus be ameliorated by past life regression.

Some people think that they can use obesity as a kind of magical protection against certain types of wasting illnesses. For example, people who are afraid of cancer often put on weight because they think that being heavy means that they are healthy. Others feel that added weight provides an insulating layer between the self and the body, dulling awareness of any perceived danger (real or imagined) and appearing to protect the heavy person from the "hard knocks" of the world.

When sexual abuse is the cause of the obesity, past life therapy can successfully treat both the symptom *and* the cause, the cause being as severe psychologically as the physical burden the symptom places on the body. The whole person is treated. There is no need to regain the weight, to repeat the process again and again. The causative trauma is no longer hidden. Simultaneously, both the inner and outer selves are healed.

For some patients, regression to childhood in the present lifetime can be enough to cure chronic and health-threatening obesity. For a brief period several years ago, I was a consultant to the Gastroenterology Division of the hospital. I interviewed patients suffering from severe obesity preliminary to their entering a research program that involved an invasive procedure to promote weight loss.

One of the patients whom I had previously interviewed was later referred back to me by a colleague. Sharon weighed 295 pounds, and like some of the other participants in the program, she had failed to lose weight. Sharon had also tried a form of hypnotherapy that employs positive suggestions to aid in weight loss, but this had not been successful for her either. Traditional psychotherapy also proved unsuccessful. Numerous diets had failed. Any weight loss had been quickly reversed as her weight ballooned back to the familiar three-hundred-pound plateau.

In childhood and adolescence, Sharon had been only ten to twenty pounds overweight. The explosion to three hundred pounds did not begin until shortly after her marriage. During their courtship, she had idealized and fallen deeply in love with her husband. Meanwhile, her subconscious mind was denying (not allowing her to see or bring into awareness) some of his less perfect personality traits, such as his compulsive flirting with other women. Soon after they were married, however, Sharon could no longer ignore reality. An affair of her husband's became public knowledge, and with this disclosure had come the onset of Sharon's severe obesity.

Hypnotic regression revealed that Sharon had been publicly humiliated in early adolescence by a teenage boy who had made fun of her developing figure. This was progress, but there was more. Tearfully and still in a trance state, Sharon recalled the original cause of her obesity. Her stepfather had fondled her when she was a little girl of four. These memories had been deeply repressed for many years.

The betrayal of her husband was the trigger, but the bullet was loaded at age four and the hammer drawn when Sharon was humiliated at age thirteen. She could not trust men. She had to be protected from them. The answer was to become so obese that no man could ever find her attractive, and, therefore, she could not be hurt again.

After this hypnosis session when she remembered her childhood sexual abuse, Sharon began to lose weight. Her voracious appetite abated, and she was able to eat sensibly. Short-term psychotherapy quickly reversed her distrust of men. Since our session, Sharon has lost 165 pounds and has maintained that loss.

Gerald Kein, a prominent hypnotherapist, has treated literally thousands of people for obesity during his professional experience of over twenty-five years. When I asked his opinion of these cases and others like them, he told me that, in his experience, posthypnotic suggestion alone—the type of hypnosis Sharon had tried before coming to me that had proved unsuccessful for her—is not successful in helping the patient achieve the desired weight loss if the patient is more than thirty or forty pounds overweight and has been obese for a long period of time.

In other words, he believes that traditional hypnosis employing direct suggestion—e.g., "You will eat only three meals a day; your stomach will feel full between meals; you will eat only foods that are nutritious"—does not successfully treat chronic obesity. The suggestions might help the patient diet and temporarily lose some weight, but the weight will nearly always come back.

However, Kein has found that regression to the *cause* of chronic obesity—whether that cause is found in significant childhood experiences or in the patient's past lives—does cure the condition. And he has also found that when obesity is successfully treated with regression therapy, the weight loss is usually permanent.

My experience with Kathy, Dee, Sharon, and other obese patients echoes Kein's observations. When the real reason for obesity can be uncovered by regression to the source, whether to childhood in this lifetime or to past life sources, the excess weight seems to simply drop off. Most of my regression patients have been able to resist any significant subsequent weight gain. If a patient does start to gain weight again, a session in which the memory is reexperienced or reviewed is often enough to reverse this trend.

This method also works for patients who have inherited tendencies toward obesity. These days, much attention is being given to the possibility that some of us may inherit certain genes that predispose us toward becoming chronically overweight. While such a genetic inheritance may indeed exist, it is important to remember that a tendency is just a tendency—it is *not* a certainty.

Past life regression gives patients the strength and also the tools to overcome any sort of tendency. Tendencies are not inevitable, irresistible, or irreversible. With past life regression and the subsequent understanding, a physical tendency can be reversed just as easily as any of the psychological ones we have discussed in these chapters.

Perhaps knowledge of the source of this cure is already deeply embedded within us. Whenever I ask an obese person how long he or she has been overweight, the answer is usually "forever."

Substance abusers are also often deeply aware of the "foreverness" of their problem. Sometimes the tendency toward substance abuse itself is one that has been carried over from previous lifetimes. Or, the problems that a person hopes can be masked by using alcohol or drugs may be the issues that have been carried over from another lifetime, giving the feeling of timelessness and eternity.

In either case, patients facing the challenge of recovery often have an underlying need in common with the obese. And that need is the need to protect.

Like excess weight, drugs and alcohol can seem to provide a layer between the person and his or her feelings, fears, and the hurts inflicted by others. Drugs can also insulate an addict from taking responsibility for his or her life because the addict can always blame the drugs or alcohol for problems. It is easy to use addiction as an excuse for failures, disappointments, or mistakes instead of accepting such setbacks realistically and using them as opportunities for growth.

In contrast to obesity, the motivation for substance abuse behavior often involves an element of escapism or avoidance. Substance abuse typically provides a method of suppressing memories or feelings.

In this sense, the dulling of awareness with drugs and alcohol can be a form of slow suicide. Like suicide, substance abuse is a way of avoiding or escaping intolerable issues. Substance abusers who undergo past life regression therapy sometimes discover that they have committed suicide in other lives and that the issues they wanted to escape from previously have resurfaced with a vengeance. This time the need to escape has been translated into the slower suicide and escapism of addiction.

In some cases, the opportunities for growth in a past lifetime were "wasted" when painful issues could not be confronted. Perhaps in that previous lifetime, significant issues were avoided through the veil of altered states induced by alcohol or drugs. Although the issues might now be different, the temptation to use the same "escape hatch" to avoid pain may have recurred.

Either way, the only way to get rid of both the core issue and the trap of substance abuse is to meet them both head-on and solve them in a spiritual and realistic manner.

Once acute intervention is accomplished, past life therapy can treat the underlying causes of addiction, which may have roots in challenging family relationships and/or prior childhood abuse. For some patients, the core issue may revolve around a theme of anger or violence, since the expression of these qualities is facilitated by alcohol and drug use. For others, core issues may involve problems in courage or self-love. Alcohol can provide a pseudo-confidence.

I rarely treat patients who are in the acute stage of an addiction to alcohol or drugs. Hypnosis is not effective when a person is under the influence of these substances. In this acute stage, a substance abuser should seek help from an inpatient intervention program or from a support group such as Alcoholics Anonymous (AA) or Narcotics Anonymous (NA). Those who come to my office have usually completed the detoxification process and are interested in healing core issues in their lives. Often, they have come to recognize that substance abuse is a symptom that has blotted out or provided escape from painful life traumas. These patients frequently recognize that their substance abuse was much more painful than the original traumatic event.

Inner child work and past life regression therapy provide a method for releasing both the primal pain and the maladaptive behavior. From the perspective of the inner child, harmful habits seem worth the price of alleviating such enormous pain. But from the adult perspective, the pain can be made to appear manageable. It can be released, and with it the need for dulling, desensitizing, and protective habits is also released.

Recovering addicts can make excellent candidates for past life therapy, because the problem of alcoholism or substance abuse is so often at the heart of a spiritual path. The reward for overcoming substance abuse is a precious one. The process may provide an accelerated path of spiritual growth. It is through understanding, faith, and wisdom that alcoholism and drug abuse are overcome.

Sarah had been an alcoholic for many years. She would also go on periodic spending sprees. However, she was not manic-depressive and did not require lithium. Careful exploration of her childhood revealed marked dysfunction in her family. She was involved in a classic codependency situation with her husband. Psychoanalysis, which had lasted eight years, had not changed her behaviors. She had failed in group therapy and in a chemical-dependency inpatient unit.

It was not until she began to explore her past lives that a dramatic improvement began. She discovered that in prior lifetimes she, her parents, and her husband had repeatedly been together in abusive, alcoholic relationships. There had been violence, murder, suicide, and all sorts of chaos and mayhem. The actual details were not as important as the recurring pattern. Sarah resolved to break the pattern, realizing that the family would be condemned to endlessly repeat this destructive play until they had learned their lessons.

"I must forgive them," she mused after recalling a previous traumatic death, ". . . and I can only do that through love. I must express my love by letting go . . . must forgive them . . . and myself."

And she did. Sarah now meditates regularly, volunteers with the severely handicapped, and no longer abuses substances or uses money for ego gratification.

Sarah's understanding of the repetitive destructive behavior patterns in herself and her family, patterns spanning lifetimes, aided in her recovery. The experience of the extremely relaxed, almost blissful state induced by the hypnotic regression also helped her. She seemed to be talking to me from a higher, more detached and more aware perspective. Sarah was neither angry, anxious, nor judgmental. She could clearly see patterns, causes and effects, roots of symptoms, manipulations, and so on. It was as if her perception of reality was much sharper.

I have found that the experience of regression therapy can be supportive of the Alcoholics Anonymous Twelve-Step recovery process. For your information, here are the Twelve Steps of the AA program:

Step One: *We admitted we were powerless over alcohol, that our lives had become unmanageable.*
Step Two: *Came to believe that a Power greater than ourselves could restore us to sanity.*
Step Three: *Made a decision to turn our will and our lives over to the care of God as we understood him.*
Step Four: *Made a searching and fearless moral inventory of ourselves.*
Step Five: *Admitted to God, to ourselves, and to another human being the exact nature of our wrongs.*
Step Six: *Were entirely ready to have God remove all these defects of character.*
Step Seven: *Humbly asked Him to remove our shortcomings.*
Step Eight: *Made a list of all persons we had harmed, and became willing to make amends to them all.*
Step Nine: *Made direct amends to such people whenever possible, except when to do so would injure them or others.*
Step Ten: *Continued to take personal inventory and when we were wrong promptly admitted it.*
Step Eleven: *Sought through prayer and meditation to improve our conscious contact with God as we understood him, praying only for knowledge of His will for us and the power to carry that out.*
Step Twelve: *Having had a spiritual awakening as a result of these steps, we tried to carry this message to alcoholics, and to practice these principles in all our affairs.*

Many of the issues addressed in past life therapy correspond to these Twelve Steps. The basis of both is spirituality. Both recognize the primacy of a higher power or plan. This does not imply a formal religious context. The power can be discovered within.

Spirituality is a vitally important force. Lives change because of it. Values change. People become less violent, greedy, self-centered. They become less afraid. Having had these experiences, they tell others, who in turn carry the same message to many more.

Ultimately, in both obesity and substance abuse and really in any form of suffering, the mechanism of healing involves the process of getting rid of fear.

The core healing mechanism of past life regression therapy is the transmutation of fear into love. This is the message of healing that those who have experienced past life regression carry to others and, hopefully, practice in all their affairs.

How do you do it? By knowing yourself. By looking within and seeing clearly. By understanding and acquiring wisdom. By becoming more joyful and peaceful. This is the essence of any past life healing.

8

Healing the Grieving

A FIFTY-FIVE-YEAR-OLD MAN WAS DYING OF METASTATIC lung cancer in a major university hospital. For a while chemotherapy had stopped the progress of his disease, but finally the lethal cancer had gained the upper hand. Leonard was waiting to die. When he could, he passed the time talking to his wife, Evelyn, or to his physicians. Fortunately, these were physicians who took the time to listen to him.

"How long will it take to die?" Leonard asked his doctor one day.

"I don't know. It could happen anytime, or it could take quite a while," the doctor answered. Then Leonard and his doctor talked about letting go and being able to die. Leonard's wife was included in this conversation, and she felt both comforted and comfortable with the words and thoughts.

The couple talked even more after this meeting. It was as though something had been unlocked and released in them. Leonard and Evelyn began to spend even more time together.

Leonard's level of alertness began to fluctuate as his terminal condition deteriorated. At times, he was semicomatose. At other moments, he was fairly alert. Evelyn thought he was having hallucinations.

"Leonard feels like he's floating," Evelyn told Leonard's doctor.

"Perhaps it's not an hallucination," the doctor replied. "Many patients tell me that. Is there more? I'm interested in hearing about these things."

With that, the oncologist had left the symbolic door open. He had let Evelyn know it was safe to tell him things like this, no matter how strange or unusual they might seem.

The next day when the doctor made his hospital rounds, Evelyn had something new to report.

"He said he was floating again, and he felt good about it. He heard people talking by the door, and he floated to them." The doctor assumed that Leonard had heard a conversation among nurses outside his room.

"No," Evelyn corrected. "They were people waiting to welcome him."

By the following day, Leonard was barely clinging to life.

"He said he was floating again," Evelyn told the doctor. "He went to the people outside the door."

Leonard nodded his agreement from the bed as Evelyn repeated the story.

"The people showed him a large book, and in it was the name he would have during his next life. It sounded like a Pakistani or Indian name. He told me his first name, but he couldn't see his last name."

Leonard roused himself. "They covered up the last name," he whispered hoarsely. "They said, 'No, you're not supposed to see this yet.' "

Later the same day, Leonard told Evelyn he saw a bus coming to take him somewhere. Then he spoke a few more words, which were barely audible.

"Dying is not a loss," Leonard whispered to his wife. "It is a part of living."

Those words proved to be this man's last. He died that afternoon.

Evelyn grieved his death, but she also felt comforted. She was certain now that Leonard's soul would continue to live after his death. And Leonard's final words had changed her own perceptions of death and dying. She felt much more peaceful about death's inevitability in her life.

She would never be as fearful of death again.

As it happens, Leonard's doctor was my youngest brother, Dr. Peter Weiss. He and his wife, Dr. Barbra Horn, are both specialists in hematology and oncology in St. Louis, Missouri. In private practice, they specialize in treating cancer. They are also both members of the clinical faculty of the Washington University School of Medicine.

Both Peter's and Barbra's lives have been altered personally and professionally by their relationships with their patients and also by the discussions they and I have had together about our own and our colleagues' experiences with life and death, experiences that have taught us more about what it truly means to die.

We are grateful to patients like Leonard and many others because their experiences give us more information and new perspectives concerning the dying process that, hopefully, we can share with other dying patients and with those who grieve for them, both to teach them and to heal them. From these patients we have learned that death does not have to be primarily an experience of fear, loss, and separation. This most challenging of life passages can also be a time of healing, expansion, and new beginnings.

Peter was treating a patient named Matthew. Matthew was a stoic, sixty-five-year-old professor who was reluctant to talk about his feelings as he was dying from a painful and rapidly advancing cancer of the pancreas. Peter and he finally began to communicate on a more personal level. Once again, Peter gave his patient a subtle indication that it would be all right to talk about anything, no matter how unusual the topic might seem.

"A strange thing *did* happen now that you mention it," the professor admitted. "An angel came by and asked if I were ready to go. I asked if I had to. The angel said no and then left."

Peter asked the professor how he knew his visitor had been an angel.

"By the bright light within and around, and by being so high up in the religious hierarchy," came the enigmatic reply.

A few days later, the angel reappeared.

"Are you ready yet?" the angel gently asked.

"Not yet," the professor replied.

The angel lingered. By this time, Matthew's cancer was advancing rapidly and he was in considerable discomfort, requiring potent analgesic medicine just to blunt the sharp edge of his pain. Yet this man still retained his mental acuity and alertness.

Matthew watched as the angel reached into his abdomen and removed what looked like a brown brick.

The pain immediately disappeared and the patient felt much better.

Then the angel left once again.

Gradually Matthew's pain returned, but so did the angel. Another brick was removed. There was now no pain at all, and all of the pain medicines were stopped. The visits from this healing angel provided this very logical, stoic man with great comfort and hope.

His clinical condition deteriorated further, and this man who had formerly been in excruciating pain died peacefully and quietly. Finally, Matthew must have answered "Yes" to the angel's question.

Most physicians and therapists know very little about death, dying, and grief. Those who have a personal experience of their own with grief understand it a bit more, but, in essence, most members of the healing professions do little more than describe the stages of death and dying and the symptoms of grief.

They do not explain what happens to those who are progressing from dying to death and beyond. They do not provide all of the tools to assuage grief. Clearly, we do not pretend to know everything about the spiritual process of dying, but experiences like Leonard's and Matthew's begin to provide such tools.

Grief therapy has to incorporate psychic events as well as spiritual thoughts. People who have had near death experiences, regressions to past lives and the in-between-lives state, out-of-body experiences and certain psychic phenomena dealing with life or consciousness outside of the body, usually do not grieve as deeply or as profoundly. They know something more than the rest. They know that consciousness never dies.

People who know that they are going to die often go through the process of mourning their own death. This process can begin as soon as the diagnosis of a terminal illness, such as metastatic cancer, is made. The dying person may experience feelings of denial, anger, and despair. Family and friends may also begin to grieve well before death occurs.

Grief can easily become clinical depression. The dying or grieving person feels despondent, hopeless, and beyond help. Psychological pain becomes acute and omnipresent. Sleep patterns, the ability to concentrate, appetite, and energy levels are all disrupted. Friends try to cheer the grief-stricken, to distract them from their despair, but to no avail.

Yet the grief of both patients and their families can be healed *before* death. As they learn about the wonderful experiences of others, such as those told in this book and elsewhere, they can begin to feel more hope. The dying and the grieving can be encouraged to communicate their experiences and insights to each other. They can talk about the possibility of being together again. They can express their love. They can more easily and more calmly accept death. A dreaded experience can be transformed into a time of honesty, sharing, love, and sometimes even humor.

Another patient of Peter's, the matriarch of a large Italian family, was dying as a result of an acute flare-up of her leukemia. Silvia was comfortable with her approaching death, which she believed was much more imminent than Peter did.

"I'm going to die on Saturday," Silvia announced one day.

"How do you know?" Peter asked.

"I just know," she answered.

When Peter entered Silvia's hospital room that Saturday morning, the whole family was crowded within. It seemed to Peter as though a scene from a play was being reenacted. A priest was present, and last rites were being administered.

At some point in the drama, the priest said, "And now there will be a message from God."

Just then, the telephone rang.

It *wasn't* God.

Everybody laughed, and the tension was broken.

Later that day, Silvia had a vivid out-of-body experience, being drawn to a beautiful, warm, and comforting light. She further described the light to Peter as three-dimensional and inviting. Perhaps there was a message from God after all.

Silvia died one week later.

Peter described another of his more memorable experiences with a dying patient and the patient's family. "There were seventeen members of a large and very close Irish family. But all of them were consumed with fear and anger as their relative's death approached. I got involved with all seventeen, teaching them about death, how to let go with love, how to say good-bye, how to accept what was happening. The transformation and healing that went on in that family were amazing. They began to talk, to hug, and to love. It touched me deeply."

Occurrences like these are often so compelling and extraordinary that frequently the patient is afraid that a counselor or physician who hears about the event will trivialize or dismiss this precious experience and consider the patient odd or strange. When the patient is reassured that it is safe to discuss these experiences, doctor-patient communication reaches a new level. The healing bond is strengthened. Both Peter and Barbra take the time to talk with and listen to their patients and their patients' families. They feel a responsibility to be with their dying patients, not only to provide excellent technical medical care, but also to offer psychological support. This provides immense satisfaction to them, gives comfort to the others, and has taught them a great deal.

"I no longer get so burned out," Peter says, "because I now know that death is a natural part of life. I still try my hardest to cure patients, but I no longer take their deaths, when inevitable, so personally or as failures."

We are on the frontiers of a new form of helping, one in which those in the helping professions are not merely able to identify the stages of grief but are also able to communicate a more spiritual, open, and enlightened understanding of the actual death experience. Hopefully, this frontier is one in which the dying, the grieving, and the caretakers will all be able to learn and grow together.

According to a 1990 poll by the Gallup Organization affiliate, The Princeton Religious Research Center, roughly half of all Americans believe in extrasensory perception. Like the extraordinary experiences that can occur during the dying process, psychic experiences concerning a departed loved one can also induce profound changes in a person's life and his or her attitude toward death and dying. Healing and growth can occur as these life-altering events are integrated. Profound grief and fear of death diminish, especially when the psychic experiences seem to be connected to "the other side."

A husband and wife, both respected physicians in Miami, came to see me in order to describe an unusual phenomenon they had both witnessed. The wife's father had recently died. About a week after his death, which had occurred in Colombia, both she and her husband saw her father's body, glowing brightly and somewhat translucent, waving to them from their bedroom door.

Both were wide awake at this time. They walked over to touch him, but when they did, their hands went right through his body.

The father waved good-bye and suddenly vanished. There were no words.

When they later compared notes, both physicians discovered that they had seen the same physical form, the same radiant body, and the same wave good-bye.

In another incident, a highly respected professor of psychiatry at the University of Miami came to talk with me after reading *Many Lives, Many Masters*.

I expected this man to be polite but skeptical, but I was surprised.

"You know," he began, "for many years I've secretly believed these parapsychological phenomena are real. Years ago my father had a vivid dream about his brother. His brother had been in apparent good health, yet he came to my father in a dream to say good-bye. 'I have to leave you now,' his brother said, 'but I'm fine. Take care of yourself.' When my father awakened in the morning, he knew that his brother had died."

A phone call had soon confirmed this intuitive feeling. During the night, the brother, who had no previous history of heart disease, had died of a massive heart attack in a city five hundred miles away.

Another interesting case came to me in a letter from a Miami businesswoman:

Though it was very difficult for me to discuss this for many years, I would like to share with you my experience with the death of a loved one. During my years in graduate school I was engaged to another graduate student for two years. We broke up and two years later I was married. During this time I was working in New York City, and I learned that he had taken a job in Los Angeles. It would be several months before I would learn that he had been killed in an automobile accident. Before I was informed through mutual friends of his untimely death, he visited me in my sleep for many weeks in a row.

Each time he would appear he was distraught, crying and confused as to where he was. He would ask me to help him; he didn't understand this limbo he found himself in and was not sure that he was dead. I was not frightened, but I was concerned about his well-being. At this time, I was still not aware that he had been killed. After several visits to a medium/spiritual counselor, I was told that the young man in question had indeed died and remained very close to me and because of this confusion, he naturally felt safe in searching me out.

I have learned in interviewing patients and conducting past life regressions that it is not rare for those suffering a sudden and violent death to cling to the earth plane and to be confused and in a state of limbo for a while. Eventually, though, they do find their way to the wonderful light and the spiritual presence of a guide or universal love and move onward.

Several other people who have come to my office have described similar visits shortly after the physical death of a loved one. Some have even described receiving phone calls from the recently deceased, calls that have sent shivers down their spines. In my professional opinion, the descriptions above and many others that I have heard come from normal, nonhallucinating people.

It seems that a primary purpose of experiences like these is to encourage the living to heal their grief through understanding. Like my brother Peter's patients, those who have these experiences come to understand that they will never die, that only their bodies will die. For death is inevitable. Death is how we grow, how we move from lesson to lesson, from lifetime to lifetime. We will all die, and based on what I have learned from past life regression therapy, most of us have already died many times before this lifetime.

This is good news. This means that most of us have grown significantly, have been allowed to savor new life experiences while retaining former strengths, talents, and even loves. It also means that we will continue to grow even after our deaths.

Martha was another patient who resolved her grief almost as a bonus of her past life therapy experience. Martha was a twenty-six-year-old film editor who said that she had no symptoms when she came to see me. She simply told me that she wanted to have a regression experience out of curiosity, to see "what came up."

The simple desire to explore and to know more is a wonderful reason to try past life therapy. Those who are suffering from symptoms are not the only ones who can benefit, grow, and become more joyful through this particular method of spiritual growth.

Martha quickly slipped into the key moment flow regression pattern. First, she saw herself as a young boy watching a hanging taking place on a platform. In this key moment Martha was being teased by her older brothers, who were making her feel quite uncomfortable. Then Martha saw her home in that lifetime, and she realized that her father in that lifetime is her deceased father in the present lifetime. Later in this past life, Martha was conscripted into the military, where she remained. She married, had an uneventful life, and finally died of old age on a stone bed. During the death experience, Martha found the light above her and flew to it, speeding through space and time with other spirits, finally merging with a golden light for her life review. During the life review, Martha commented that the day on which she had seen the hanging had been a very important one for her, for on that day she had learned about the difference between good and evil and about the futility of violence, despite the fact that at the time her primary concern had been that of being teased by her brothers.

As Martha moved on to another lifetime, she saw herself as an old man dressed in what seemed to be a toga. She had a white beard and was playing music on a lyre. This was her only memory of that lifetime although she had a very clear impression that the entire lifetime had been a very happy one. In the third lifetime that Martha recalled, she was a woman with dark hair and green eyes. In this lifetime Martha had been the mother of two babies who gave her a great deal of joy.

After the session was over, we spent time integrating Martha's experience. Martha told me how great she felt to have remembered having lived three lifetimes filled with joy and happiness. She said that the regression helped her quite a bit. As a young person still at the beginning of adult life, Martha was also relieved that she could call on her happy past lifetimes to create lasting happiness in this lifetime. This seemed more real and tangible to her, less abstract.

But Martha also told me that, to her surprise, the experience had helped her heal a longstanding, lingering feeling of grief and mourning over the death of her father four years previously. It had also helped her clarify her own understanding of death. She now knew that she had known him before, and, of course, that she herself had lived before. The possibility existed that they could meet again. Her experience had proved to her that death as a final ending does not exist. Her father might no longer be with her physically, but she felt uplifted to know that his consciousness lived on.

For Martha, resolving her grief was an unexpected bonus of this process. However, other patients specifically seek past life regression for this purpose.

Rena is a twenty-eight-year-old social policy lawyer. She was married to a prominent newspaper columnist in his thirties. Only several years after their marriage, Rena's husband tragically discovered that he was suffering from terminal cancer. During Jim's illness, he and Rena had many arguments about life after death and the existence of other realities. Rena had a strong belief in both, but Jim was extremely skeptical.

Trained as a journalist with superior reasoning skills, he had a professional bias for not accepting the existence of anything that he could not verify factually. Jim not only refused to consider these possibilities for himself, but he had also tried to wear down Rena's personal faith in life after death and the immortality of the soul, which was one of her greatest comforts and supports as she began to grieve her husband's imminent loss. As Jim's condition deteriorated, their arguments continued. Jim appeared to become angrier and angrier, both about his condition and about Rena's beliefs. He also seemed to become more and more fearful.

Finally, Jim was hospitalized. Both he and Rena knew his death was imminent. Right before Jim's death, though, something astonishing happened. He calmly told Rena that he had seen an old man sitting in a chair in his room, and that the old man had told him he was there waiting to take him on his journey. He added that she had been right about this subject all along, that he had been wrong. He apologized for being so recalcitrant and hoped she would continue to explore and learn more after his death.

After he reported this news to the astonished Rena, this formerly angry, agitated, and fearful man became peaceful about his impending death.

Jim died the next day.

When Rena came to see me, she told me that she herself was very grateful to have reconciled with Jim on this important and formerly divisive matter before his death. The wonderful change that the appearance of the old man had wrought in Jim had also been healing for Rena. It had brought her confirmation of her own beliefs, and to receive confirmation in such difficult and important circumstances had been a very precious gift.

Rena's visit to me had many reasons. She was still suffering from some grief and anxiety at her unexpected and recent loss. She needed to integrate this important death experience further, not only the grieving but also the profound growth and healing that had begun to blossom in her at the same time. And Rena's visit to my office was also part of her fulfillment of the promise she had made to Jim that she would continue to study and explore life after death, spirituality, and the immortality of the soul.

Interestingly, Rena's regression experience did not directly address her relationship to Jim. Instead, Rena's past life memories seemed to give her a message about another fresh and ripe new field of learning and growth.

Rena regressed to a lifetime in which she had been a male Native American who had helped nurse and cure sick Pilgrim children in the seventeenth century. After the session, Rena recalled that as a child she had always picked school projects that had to do with the Pilgrims and she had always seemed to know a lot about them.

With the regression session completed, Rena felt that she had now experienced her own immortality firsthand. More significantly, the regression seemed to unveil heretofore unknown talents in Rena's own past, talents that she might be able to develop once again in this lifetime.

Whether this includes health care, work with children, or a

sensitivity to certain aspects of early American history remains to be seen. The subconscious, inner wisdom that led Rena to access that particular lifetime might also be giving her conscious self a message that Rena herself had helped Jim face his dying and his death.

What is certain is that this session, intended to help her resolve her grief, had, like Jim's death itself, furthered Rena's growth and surprised her with yet another clue to her evolving understanding of herself. It had pointed to the many new directions and experiences that might still lie ahead of her.

Jim's and Rena's experience is a very profound example of the potential for growth and healing that the death experience contains. Many of the dying report being visited by a guide or a wise person who is waiting for them. The alertness of the patient does not seem to be a factor. Whether the patient is alert or not, in a chemically medicated state or not, these experiences must not be dismissed as mere hallucination. If a loved one tells you of such an experience right before death, you can let go of your doubt and feel fairly confident that the experience is real.

Philip was a computer software designer who also sought the past life regression process in order to heal his grief. Philip and his wife, Eva, had lost two very young children, a girl and a boy, to a rare congenital birth defect at the ages of three and four. Perhaps the most tragic aspect of Philip's children's story was the fact that the loss of a second child might have been prevented. After their first child, their daughter, was diagnosed, Philip and Eva had been told that the defect was *not* hereditary and therefore there was no reason they should not have a second, healthy child. However, this advice was inaccurate, and Philip and Eva had to suffer again the loss of a child, this time with the knowledge that the tragedy and their son's suffering could have been avoided. Feelings of responsibility, loss, and grief were inextricably and devastatingly intertwined.

The tragedy was several years behind Philip when he came for therapy, but he was still mourning. As a computer scientist with advanced graduate degrees, Philip was highly trained to use logical, analytic reasoning, but he also had a strong Catholic background, and this orientation had made him quite comfortable with a full range of spiritual phenomena and experiences as well. Several times since the children's deaths, Philip had visited a famous psychic who seemed to be able to communicate with his little boy and his little girl. He had grasped at this opportunity to resolve his grief, and he felt that his sessions with this medium had been helpful. But the psychic had recently died. Philip felt that now he had no chance of contact with his children, and this lack of contact had deepened his grief.

Based on the results I have observed with other patients, it seemed that a regression experience might give him a new perspective to deal with his losses.

Philip proved to be a good subject for hypnosis. He was soon in a deep and relaxed trance state, and he appeared to be having a vivid past life experience. He described being in a beautiful alpine meadow high in the mountains, surrounded by a profusion of wildflowers in full bloom. Suddenly, he saw his children, now older, approaching him. They ran to him and danced around him, laughing and singing. Then Philip's deceased father and mother joined them, along with his maternal grandfather, to whom Philip had been especially close.

First Philip's children, and then his parents and grandfather, came and held his hands. Philip could describe the touch of his children's hands in his, how real the feeling was, how strong their grip, how much stronger they now were, and how much they had grown. Looking into his eyes, all of them communicated with him deeply. They told him that they loved him. They told him not to worry, that everything was fine, and that they were fine. They were very happy in this meadow and in this dimension. Joy literally sparkled from their eyes and their smiles.

Clearly, despite the vividness of the surroundings, this was not a past life experience at all. In trance, Philip seemed to have entered another dimension.

Even before we began the integration process for the session, it was obvious that Philip's experience had been emotionally cathartic. He told me how happy he was to have had this direct experience of contact with his children. As he described the sensation of their hands holding his, he literally began to cry with joy. Philip's experience in the meadow finally allowed him to release the guilt, grief, and helplessness that had burdened him for so many years. He gained an understanding of the immortality of the soul, and he began to anticipate a life of renewed purpose and optimism.

Since this regression session, Philip continues to feel joyful. The burden that he carried for so many years has not reappeared.

Critics may comment that reunions such as these consist of nothing more than fantasy or wish fulfillment. But fantasy and wish fulfillment do not produce the powerful healing forces that can take place as a patient reconnects with the eternal nature of the soul and experiences bonds with departed loved ones. Martha, Rena, and Philip all felt dramatically better after their trance experiences and all reported that ongoing symptoms of grief and anxiety lifted as a result.

Everyone whose story has been told in this chapter has learned that death is not absolute. Ultimately, it is this knowledge that is the great healer. The loved one is not lost. After death, a connection to that person remains.

People who have this experience or knowledge learn that death is less of an ending than a transition. It is like walking through a door into another room. Depending on the level of spiritual or psychic development or interest, communication with someone in that next room may be very clear, or intermittent, or there may be no communication at all. Nonetheless, whatever the nature of the basic connection, it can be improved as long as the grieving understand that the separation is not permanent or absolute. Like Martha and her father, they and their loved ones have probably been together before, and separated before. Yet, they were allowed to come together again. Like Philip, they learn that the consciousness of the loved one has only died in physical form.

This gives the grieving great hope for the future, hope that they will meet again. Of course, they may not meet within the same relationships or circumstances that prevailed in the current lifetime. For example, a father and daughter might meet again as friends or siblings or grandfather and grandchild. Nevertheless, souls do continue to meet again and again.

In a way, the grief of the dying is a grief over loss of self, and in that sense, the past life regression experience can also be very helpful. Those who experience it or learn of it understand that death doesn't mean a disappearance of the self into oblivion or blackness. Patients have shown me that it simply means that, in the wisdom of the soul, the body is no longer needed. The time has come for the soul to pass out of the body and to exist in a nonphysical, spiritual state. Awareness is immortal, and so are aspects of the personality.

Often the soul returns to a new lifetime with the same talents and abilities a person exhibited in a previous lifetime. Sometimes, people even access unknown talents in the current lifetime after recalling the existence of these talents in previous lives.

There are so many different levels of the self. We are wonderful, multidimensional beings. Why must we limit ourselves mentally by restricting our definition of ourselves to the personality and body that exists in the here and now? The entire spirit is not encapsulated in the body and the conscious mind. The part of the self that exists here is, in all probability, just a fragment of the entire spirit.

No doubt the potential exists that even as Philip met his children in the meadow, another aspect of his son's and daughter's souls could be growing and expanding further in a new incarnation. The versatility and potential of the soul are limitless, infinite. The ideas and experiences outlined in this chapter are probably just the tip of the iceberg in terms of the ability to account for the full dimensions of the soul.

The mystic Yogananda has said that life is like a long golden chain floating deep within an ocean. It can only be pulled out and examined one link at a time while the rest glistens beneath the surface, alluring and unobtainable. What we now know of death, indeed of life and the soul, is probably just one link in this golden chain. As we integrate our grief into growth, we will be able to raise more and more of this golden chain of joy and wisdom from the ocean of being and into the light.

9

Opening the Mind to the Power of Mystical Experiences

RECENTLY, I WAS A GUEST ON A RADIO TALK SHOW IN Cleveland. Listeners called in from their homes, offices, car phones, and pay phones. Many of them were very supportive as they shared their personal experiences with me, with the talk show host, and with the other program listeners. Others were less kind. One lady was very angry.

"Don't you know it's a sin?" she hissed.

I assumed that she was referring to the concept of reincarnation. She wasn't.

"Hypnosis is a sin," she went on. "Jesus said it's sinful. Devils can enter your body!"

I knew that Jesus hadn't said anything about hypnosis. The word hadn't been in usage then. Hypnosis wasn't used as a therapeutic tool until at least the eighteenth century, around the time of Mesmer. However, I take every question and comment seriously. Perhaps she was referring to some similar state of altered consciousness, or focused concentration, even if the actual word *hypnosis* hadn't yet been coined.

I thought for a moment or two.

"If hypnosis is a sin," I ventured, "why does the Archdiocese of Miami send us nuns, priests, and employees for hypnosis?"

Granted, these people were not being sent to us for regression therapy. But for over a decade we had been using hypnosis to help them to stop smoking, to lose weight, or to lessen stress.

The woman was silent for a few seconds as she pondered this new piece of information. Then she spoke up again, without conceding an inch.

"I don't know about Miami," she confidently went on, "but it's a sin in Cleveland!"

The show host looked over at me, barely suppressing a laugh. We had just been introduced to the concept of regional sin.

Why was the lady in Cleveland so angry? She was afraid because the idea of hypnosis was a new one for her, and it had threatened her concept of the way things ought to be. I had challenged her view of reality, her understanding of the world. I had scared her. At least she was honest.

When I tell this story at my workshops, it always gets a big laugh. But some of that laughter is the laughter of self-recognition, recognition of having one's view of reality, one's understanding of the world, challenged by a new idea or concept. And that idea might turn out to be a very important one. In fact, probably all of us have come up against at least one such concept in our lifetime, although it might be a different one for each of us. And all of us have benefited from new and threatening ideas that were presented at one time or another in history.

History is the best teacher of the growth that can be gained if we can overcome our fear of certain new ideas. Some of these ideas have opened vast new paths in science, economics, politics, literature, and the arts. Some of them have accessed new geographies and remapped space. Ideas have greatly expanded the inner boundaries of what our ancestors could achieve, feel, know, and understand.

In 1633, Galileo was tried by the Inquisition for proposing a theory, based on his direct scientific experience and observation with a telescope of his own creation, that the earth rotated on its own axis around the sun. The sun only *appeared* to rotate around the earth. Thus Galileo refuted the long-held theory of the geocentric universe.

Heresy! said the Church, and Galileo was locked up in a tower. In order to be released, this brilliant scientist, who had become a professor of mathematics at the prestigious University of Pisa at the age of twenty-five, was forced to recant. Only then was he set free.

Isaac Newton, who was born on the day of Galileo's death in 1642, availed himself of the Pisan's work to develop his own theory of a mechanistic universe, one that worked through physical forces and without divine intervention.

Newton's work was accepted, and humanity's perception of the working of the universe was forever changed. Despite the Church's best efforts, Galileo's work was eventually accepted and highly praised. Today, every school child reads about him, not only because of the importance of his scientific work, but also for the way he demonstrated that people find the truth by going within and trusting their own thoughts and experiences, not by relying on what other people tell them is true. Galileo's work opened the way to new vistas in science, religion, and intellectual and cultural history. His work changed the way we all view reality.

For the lady in Cleveland, the acceptance of the idea that hypnosis can heal might be equally dramatic. It might be a key that opens the door to many types of growth for her personally. Many of us may someday stumble across an idea that serves the same purpose in our own lives. Earlier in this book, I talked about the role of the mind in preparing ourselves for the regression experience, but sometimes the mind plays more than a minor role in past life regression. Sometimes, during therapy, we discover it is a central player in the healing process. No matter how prepared we are, we may discover that an opening of our minds and the transformation of fears and limitations into empowerment and joy are the central lessons.

For many of us, the regression experience includes the realization that something you were told when you were young, and perhaps have been struggling with, just isn't true.

The uncomfortable belief may be a religious teaching, or it may be an idea about the nature of the universe, or it may concern science or perhaps something else entirely. No matter what it is, as a result of your regression experience you may find that this belief has interfered with your own experience of truth. You may also discover that this belief somehow interferes, perhaps in the smallest, most subtle way, with your personal growth and power or capacity for joy. As a result of releasing this contradictory belief, the old way of looking and thinking about things goes away.

How did you acquire this limiting belief in the first place? The person who told you might have been wrong. Or, you might have accepted what you were taught when you were quite young without thinking it through yourself or having your own confirming experiences. But that does not change the truth. Truth is absolute, and truth, like love, is constant.

When you accept the truth, life's possibilities seem to expand. The lesson for some people is to open up to truth and love.

Anita was a forty-two-year-old housewife from a strong Italian Catholic cultural and religious background. When she came to me "just to see what comes up," she was severely depressed and taking medication for this depression. Anita exhibited the usual symptoms of a clinical depression—dysphoric mood, disordered sleep, feelings of hopelessness and despair, and a lack of energy. This condition usually indicates a feeling of powerlessness, and this word certainly described Anita. She felt oppressed by her family, her ritualistically religious background, and especially by the way these two forces seemed to dictate her role in life.

In our initial interview, Anita behaved very deferentially and timidly, but at the same time she did manage to confess that she felt claustrophobic and stuck. She was particularly depressed about her relationship with her father, who persisted in behaving in a demanding and authoritarian way toward his adult daughter.

Anita resented the limitations made by her father's demands on her life, but at the same time she felt guilty about her own anger.

Anita felt unable to confront her father and remedy the situation because of the strict filial obedience her Catholicism demanded. She was afraid that if she challenged his treatment of her, she would no longer be able to consider herself a good Catholic.

Because Anita was a deeply religious woman, the prospect of rejecting or distancing herself "from God" in any way was extremely distressing. The strain between her need for her religion and her need to fulfill her own needs had created a psychological trigger for an inherited biological disposition toward depression, which was exacerbated by her relationship with her father. And, on top of that, Anita was very disturbed that her religion did not accept reincarnation, a concept she believed in quite strongly and that had brought her to my office.

Although I had no specific expectations for the session, it would not have been unusual for Anita to have entered a lifetime that addressed power. It might have been one in which she abused power, resulting in her current timidness and depressive submission to authority, or it might have been one that mirrored or somehow elucidated either the current "powerless" situation or her experience with her father.

However, as we began the regression, an unusual thing happened. When she opened the door to the past, Anita did not enter a past life. Instead, she went to a place that seemed to be between lives. It appeared to be a gardenlike place filled with much wisdom. It pulsed with purple and golden light, and it was filled with many wise guides. Suddenly, from that place, this withdrawn and deferential woman began to teach me profound truths about love and wisdom.

"When you want to comfort someone, don't listen to their words; the words may be misleading or wrong," Anita calmly advised me. "Go straight to their heart, straight to their hurt. Their words may be pushing you away, but they still need comforting."

When I heard these words, I was amused. Other patients, accessing a similar place, had echoed these same thoughts. This woman, who was not a scholar, a theologian, a philosopher, or psychologist, was nevertheless teaching me something very important about human nature.

Anita had more to say. She went on to utter another beautiful thought fragment from the between-lives state:

" . . . An alignment of love from the mind to love from the heart. Then we're in harmony, in balance."

Anita had just uttered something very close to a classic esoteric definition of wisdom, which involves the blending of the mind and heart. Here was a woman who, without any background or training in this philosophy, had spontaneously begun teaching wisdom.

When Anita returned from her relaxed, altered state, she was deeply affected by her mystical experience. Some very interesting changes resulted. The powerlessness she felt began to diminish, replaced by a feeling of personal empowerment and strength. Her depression gradually lifted and has not recurred. Now that she has had her own experience of truth, she feels less oppressed by her perception of traditional Catholic values. She is more confident about redefining her relationship with her father, a task that she has undertaken with gusto. She feels more love toward him now because her regression experience allowed her to understand deeply and personally the important part love plays in grace.

She is also able to see her father more clearly as a person with his own fears and limitations. He has become life-sized, and she has forgiven him.

Anita recently confided to me that her experience with accessing truth directly has resulted in an unexpected "bonus." She has discovered that she has some healing abilities. For instance, she has found that her children's fevers respond to her touch. She has met with some well-known healers and feels that she is at the very beginning of a long, wonderful, and exciting path.

Born with congenital heart defects, a young boy required open-heart surgery at ages three months, two and one-half years, and again at five years. The boy nearly died several times during the operations, and his doctors did not expect him to survive. When he was eight years old, he revealed to his mother that while still unconscious after one of the surgeries, he had been visited in the intensive care unit by "eight Chinese guys" who conveyed information about his recovery. The boy observed that one of the Chinese men "had a sword that he was always twirling around." This man frequently cut off his beard with the sword, but the beard grew back almost immediately. The boy described all eight "Chinese guys" in detail.

In researching her son's startling story, his mother found the physical and philosophical representation of her son's "eight Chinese guys." They are the Pa Hsien or Eight Immortals, Taoist representations of historical figures who have attained immortality. As her son described, one of these is Lu Tung-Pin, the patron saint of barbers, who was granted a magic sword as a reward for overcoming ten temptations.

The boy claims that he is still visited by the "eight Chinese guys," who continue to provide him with information. This is his direct mystical experience of truth and guidance, which he accepts completely, joyfully, and unquestioningly and which provides him with comfort in traumatic and frightening moments. Unencumbered with an adult's mental filter of what is "right" and "wrong" to think and believe, this child is able to accept both a direct source of guidance and a direct experience of spirituality. Unlike his very curious and well-intentioned mother, he has no need to research the facts.

I recently had a patient from Georgia. Beth was a woman in her early fifties who ran a real estate business out of her home. She had been separated from her extremely controlling husband, who had been having an affair. At the same time, she recognized that she was overinvolved with her adult children's lives. As a result of the separation from her husband, which was a positive step for Beth personally, she had taken on her daughter's and son's problems in relationships and careers as if they were her own. Beth felt the need to overcompensate for her husband's aloofness to the children, and this added responsibility compounded her other problems, causing her to feel depressed and overwhelmed.

Beth was unfamiliar with esoteric literature. She had read *Many Lives, Many Masters*, but little else about psychic phenomena, past lives, or related subjects. Most of all, she was concerned about her relationships and alleviating her feelings of sadness and hopelessness.

In an hypnotic state, Beth began to relate an episode that made me recall what I had read about Edgar Cayce, the legendary medium and seer.

Beth found herself in a magical garden or estate filled with beautiful rolling lawns and hillsides and dotted with unusual-looking crystalline structures or buildings. Soon she stopped in front of a large and particularly beautiful building that was inlaid with marble.

At this point, a wise guide wearing a white robe joined her. Together they ascended the staircase that led to the building. Beth had the feeling that these steps were vaguely familiar. Once inside, she discovered that this building had many rooms in it, like a library.

Her guide showed her a large room and led her to a particular shelf, where she found a book that had her name on the spine. She opened it to a page that had the circumstances of her current lifetime written on it. Beth found that if she turned back the pages in the book, she could read about her past lifetimes, and she did so. I watched her scan the book with her eyes closed. She seemed to be experiencing and absorbing quite a bit, but she did not feel the need to share this knowledge with me. Beth was told that other pages in the book held her future lifetimes, but, in very loving tones, her guide asked her not to look at those pages. In the book, Beth also found what she called her soul name. After an hour's "visit," she reluctantly returned.

The depressed and saddened woman who had entered my office had disappeared. She began to reassure me about how beautiful and loving this experience was, and her demeanor showed me that she was full of hope, that there was nothing left of her fear.

She related that she was told she had been to this place before, but that the time hadn't been right. That was why the steps seemed familiar. In the book, she read why she had chosen to experience her current lifetime. Her current troubles and obstacles were not random or accidental but had been designed to accelerate her spiritual progress. These challenges, her guide told her, would teach her about love, jealousy, and anger. It was in the difficult lifetimes that the most growth and progress were achieved. Easy lifetimes, she was told, were more like a "rest."

Like Anita, Beth was apparently having a mystical experience. She had gone to the place where souls rest, reflect, and regenerate between one lifetime and another, a place that is described in great detail in *Life Between Life*, by Joel L. Whitton, M.D., Ph.D., and Joe Fisher. In this place, a soul may appear before a few guides, review the lifetime that has just taken place, and decide what lifetime to experience next.

As she spoke, it was clear to me that Beth didn't know exactly what book or records she was reading. She was not conscious that she was going through the esoteric life review process. She was simply receiving the answers she needed, which, in this case, were not based on past relationships but on spiritual lessons. Now I saw that the real question Beth had been asking when she came to see me was, "Why did I choose this difficult lifetime?"

Through this unusual regression experience, Beth had found her answer. She had also gained a greater perspective and a special understanding of spirituality.

It is true that overcoming obstacles and difficulties accelerates spiritual progress. The most serious lifetime difficulties, like severe psychiatric illness or physical disability, may be signs of life progress, not regress. In my opinion, it is often the very strongest souls who have chosen to shoulder these burdens because they provide great opportunities for growth. If a lifetime can be likened to a year in school, then lifetimes such as these can be likened to a year in graduate school. This is probably why difficult lifetimes are more frequently recalled during regressions. The easier lifetimes, the "rest" periods, are usually not as significant.

Beth had achieved a new serenity and power in her own life and the ability to pursue future growth. Her mental perception of reality had deeply changed, and her perception of her own potential and ability to experience joy had expanded dramatically.

Sometimes, overcoming our fear to communicate new ideas to the world is what brings us joy. My first experience with a vivid past life recollection occurred during a series of acupressure massage treatments for chronic back and neck pain.

A few months before *Many Lives, Many Masters* was published, I went to an acupressure (shiatsu) therapist because of this recurrent pain. The sessions were conducted in silence, and I used this quiet time to meditate. An hour into my third session, I had reached a very deep state of relaxation. As the therapist was working on my feet, I was startled by an awareness of a scene from another time. I was awake, not sleeping. I knew where my body was, but I was watching and reexperiencing a movie beyond my mind.

In this scene, I was taller and thinner, with a small, dark, pointed beard. Wearing a multicolored robe, I was standing on an outside level of a strange building, examining the plants. Looking into the eyes of this thin man, I knew that I was this person. I felt his emotions. I could see through his eyes. I did not know if this was fantasy or not, but I kept watching, observing, witnessing.

It was an ancient time. The man was a priest, a powerful member of the religious hierarchy. The building was distinctly geometric, flat on the top with a larger wide bottom and sloping sides. There were seven or eight levels, with plants growing on and over the sides. Wide stairs connected the levels at certain points. I saw myself examining the plants and thought, "These plants seem tropical, but they're not plants found in Miami." Many were large and green, and I had never seen them before. Gradually, I became aware of a word in my mind: *ziggurat*. I did not know what this word meant.

I looked again at the priest, flipping back and forth from his perspective and vision to an outside, detached, overall perspective. I became aware of his life and that his earlier idealism and spirituality had given way to material values as he ascended to a position of great power and authority. He even had the ear of the royal family. Instead of using his position to promote spiritual values, brotherhood, and peacefulness in his people, he used his power for greed, sex, and to obtain even more power. I felt sad. What a waste. All those years of idealistic purpose, study, and struggle thrown away for powerful but mundane longings.

The priest died as an old man, never recapturing the virtues and idealism of his youth. He had to leave behind his wealth, power, position, and body. I again felt a great sadness. A great opportunity had been wasted.

Later that evening, I remembered the word again: *ziggurat*. I researched it in the encyclopedia. Ziggurat is the name for temples of the same geometric shape that I had visualized, temples from the Babylonian-Assyrian era. The Hanging Gardens of Babylon is an example of a ziggurat. I was shocked! I could not remember ever studying this.

A few years after this experience, I had organized a four-day regression training workshop in Boca Raton. About thirty therapists, mostly psychiatrists and psychologists from all over the country, attended. We worked for eight to twelve hours each day as all attending regressed each other and were regressed in turn. A closed system like this one, full of bright people and highly charged with energy, can become very intense, and that intensity affected me.

It affected me so much, in fact, that on the second night I woke up in the middle of a vivid dream. Once I was awake, the dream further unfolded as I continued to maintain a deep hypnagogic state.

This dream was one that tapped a past life memory. In that lifetime, I appeared as a prisoner somewhere in Europe during the Middle Ages. I was held captive in what looked like a dungeon. The room was underground and made of stone. I was chained to the wall by one arm, and I was being tortured for my beliefs, particularly for teaching about reincarnation, which was not accepted in this Catholic country. My torturer's heart was not in his task, but he followed his orders. After several days of this torture, I died.

When the dream ended, I was still in the hypnagogic state. In this highly creative state, I remembered the lifetime I had experienced several years earlier when I was a powerful priest at the ziggurat in the ancient Near East and had abused my power for material gratification. And then a voice came to me.

"When you had the chance to teach the truth, you didn't," the voice said gently and lovingly. "Then, when you didn't have the chance, you did. In that lifetime, you died for this belief when you didn't need to. You could have just as easily and successfully taught about love. At that moment, it wasn't right to force the issue. This time," the voice went on just as gently, addressing my current lifetime, "get it right."

At that moment, I understood that part of my life's purpose was that of transforming fear into love and wisdom. I could not be afraid to teach.

Caught in the rut of everyday life, we are all sometimes so consumed with worry and anxiety, so concerned with our status, our exteriors, with what others think of us, that we forget our spiritual selves, our absolute truth, our inner power. We worry so much about our reputations and positions, about being manipulated by others for their "gain" and our "loss," about appearing stupid, that we sometimes lose the courage to be spiritual. We become too fearful to know and to experience our own love and power.

Times are changing. Scientists with bold new ideas are no longer being imprisoned the way Galileo was. The struggle now is more internal and personal. The boundary between intellectual concept and direct mystical experience is blurring.

Recently, some physicists at a prominent university contacted me. They were working with a Chinese Taoist master to see if they could discover a way to map, explain, and replicate the art of Qi Gong, which promotes healing through movements, meditation, and energy work. This was a marriage of Eastern mysticism and Western science. I was invited there to explain the past life regression process, which is an essential component of the Qi Gong healing modality. With my arrival these open-minded physicists began to address the idea of reincarnation as well.

Many such dialogues are now occurring throughout the country. Physicists and psychiatrists are becoming the mystics of the nineties. We are confirming what prior mystics intuitively knew: that we are all divine beings. We have known this for thousands of years, but we have forgotten. And to know our power and return home, we have to remember what is really true. We have to remember the way.

10

Enriching Your Life

BLAIR WAS A VERY WEALTHY AND ATTRACTIVE WOMAN who sought therapy to help her deal with her marital problems. She felt that her husband was undermining her, causing her to feel powerless.

In regression, Blair remembered being a Native American male belonging to a Great Plains tribe. She recalled a day in her life as this Native American in which she was alone, walking northward in the deep white powder of a fresh snowfall. Blair described the crunching sound her feet made in the snow, how at one she felt with nature and her surroundings, and how peaceful she was savoring the simple act of walking through this landscape, moment by moment. She relished the complete and perfect solitude.

As the walk through the snow continued, Blair marveled at this person's strength, knowledge of nature, sense of balance, harmony, power, and beauty. She began to appreciate his ability to become absorbed in the natural flow of things and the pleasure this brought.

As we integrated this memory after the regression, Blair recognized that this sense of freedom and the other attendant qualities were exactly what she needed in her current life situation. She could make herself happy; she could revel in solitude. Her contentment was not dependent on her husband, and she was just as strong and self-sufficient as he. These attributes were no longer hypothetical to Blair. She had experienced them. Whether purely a past life memory or one amplified by metaphor, it allowed her to tap into the strongest and freest part of herself, in the process allowing her to transcend what she perceived as the limiting circumstances of her life.

Although past life therapy can heal significant physical and emotional problems quickly and deeply, it is not necessary to have a serious problem to benefit from this process. Many productive, highly functioning people suffering from seemingly minor problems and worries can also profit.

Felice, an attractive woman in her early thirties, also had symptoms that were not acutely dramatic but that, nonetheless, significantly influenced her quality of life. Felice suffered from low self-esteem and loss of confidence. She was also afraid of the dark. In regression, she recalled an ancient lifetime in which she had been an ugly and deformed girl who lived in a cave with her clan. She had been taunted and rejected by her community because of her appearance, and she had suffered from severe loneliness as a result. Felice recalled how she had spent much of her time huddled in the farthest and darkest recesses of the cave so that no one could see her. Eventually, this physical outcast died at a young age.

That lifetime obviously bore a relationship to her current low self-esteem. Felice had brought forward some of the pain and the poor self-image of that time, although there no longer was a physical basis for it. That lifetime also seemed to explain Felice's fear of the dark.

Once Felice understood these sources of her symptoms, her poor self-image and her confidence levels both improved.

Hank was a young man who seemed to have it all. A successful attorney in his late twenties with a significant income, he also had all-American good looks and athletic abilities, and he was quite popular with women. Overall, Hank functioned quite well in the world. However, he came to therapy reporting lack of satisfaction, malaise, and periodic depression and anxiety. Hank felt as though his life lacked a real purpose.

In regression therapy, Hank accessed a memory from the year 1874. In that lifetime, he had been a freed black slave. The memory was nothing more than a brief, fragmentary key moment, but it was a vivid one. In it, Hank was confined in a dark woodshed, and he was being whipped across the back by an unknown authority.

Despite its brevity, the experience affected him deeply. Although this memory did not provide earth-shattering illumination of the current specifics of Hank's life, he thought that it did shed light on some old shadows in his life history, such as an unusual degree of teenage rebelliousness.

After the session, Hank felt much better. Having the experience of recalling a past life seemed to give Hank a new sense of direction. The malaise and unhappiness evaporated. Although the outer circumstances of his life, already good ones, did not change, he was more content, knowing that his life contained a higher wisdom. He realized that the circumstances and events of his current lifetime have a purpose and that death will not end it.

Past life therapy can unleash sources of hidden strength, as Blair discovered. Like Felice, many people can benefit from past life therapy's ability to pinpoint the source of distortions in self-perception. And Hank's case shows how, in offering a direct, personal experience of spirituality and higher wisdom, past life therapy can replace vague feelings of lack of purpose and unhappiness with a new sense of serenity and direction.

If you have a creative block, past life therapy can sometimes reveal the prior life source of the block as it also removes it, leaving you with a new avenue of creativity, empowerment, and play.

Tricia is a well-known political talk show host. She is very successful at a demanding and high-pressured job. She is also popular and well liked. Tricia wanted to write a book. However, this intelligent and flexible woman who ad-libbed on a dime was unable to sit down and let words flow onto a page. She sought therapy to help her resolve her writer's block.

Tricia's regression was to a lifetime as a male somewhere in Europe several centuries ago. For many years, this person had been a tax collector who used a quill pen to record information in a thick book. One day, a poor woman dressed in burlap came to see the tax collector, accompanied by her many hungry children. The woman begged him to forgive her tax debt. She needed the money to feed her starving family.

Because the tax collector was afraid of the consequences if he overlooked the debt—losing his job and becoming impoverished himself—he had simply continued to write in the thick book. However, this man had always regretted making this decision.

Tricia was able to connect this memory to positive qualities in her present life, including her zeal for social justice. She could also connect her present creative block now to the fact that her writing had caused so much pain in the earlier life.

Not only did the session give Tricia more insight into herself, but she was able to start writing her book.

I once regressed a famous musician who had become unable to create new material. As a result, this performer made fewer appearances and no new recordings.

It took us one session to fix the problem.

The musician quickly entered a deep hypnotic state and vividly recalled an Irish lifetime in the nineteenth century. He had been talented then, too, but he had been severely punished for neglecting his studies, as well as for exceeding the talents and abilities of his father and older brother. It was a Catch-22. He did not have the strength or the courage to resist his family, upon whom he was too dependent for material comforts and social position. Thus, he did not pursue his talent, his passion, his joy.

Years passed. Increasingly despondent, the young man finally broke away and set sail for America, but he died en route as the result of an epidemic that had broken out on the ship.

We discussed that lifetime from the higher perspective of his superconscious self after his death aboard ship. He was still deeply hypnotized.

"I wasted my life," he observed. "I should have had the courage and the faith to pursue my talent. I did not love myself enough, and I valued the wrong things in that lifetime. I gave up because of fear, not because I loved my family. I feared rejection. They would have loved me anyway, but I didn't realize this. And it was their fears that caused them to hold me back. They also need to learn about love. Love is everything."

After he emerged from the hypnotic state, he seemed to be deeply moved by his experience. His creative block quickly disappeared, and he began to perform brilliantly and much more frequently.

Dr. Robert Jarmon had a fascinating case involving a young, well-functioning business executive who became inexplicably anxious and fearful whenever the moon was full. The reason for this fear turned out to be more complicated than gravity, tidal effects, or fluid balances.

Dr. Jarmon regressed this patient to an incident when, as a youth, the patient had to turn down a joy ride with some friends because he had to work the evening shift as a gas station attendant. The joy-riding friends had a serious accident, and two of them were killed. The moon had been full on that tragic night. The youth's grief and guilt seemed linked to that memory of the moon. Dr. Jarmon began to explain therapeutically that the accident was in the past, that the grieving and other internalized memories and feelings could now be released.

The hypnotized patient interrupted him.

"They might catch us. We have to be very careful. The moon is full tonight."

Much to Dr. Jarmon's surprise, his patient had spontaneously gone back to a lifetime as an American soldier in Europe during World War II. The soldier was caught by the Germans. His last memory was of being shot in the back as he faced a river, the moonlight reflecting up from the water's surface.

The patient was able to give his past life name during this incarnation as the soldier. He also provided the date, branch location, and site of his college graduation in the late 1930s. The patient's wife later did some research and was able to confirm that a man with that same name had indeed been graduated from that particular branch of that college. The date was off by one year.

After this regression and the memory of his death as a soldier, his strange reaction to the full moon disappeared.

Perhaps "lunacy" and much of the folklore surrounding the often profound and strange effects of the full moon on our psyches have some roots in our ancient memories. After all, we have all been looking up at the full moon for thousands of years.

Ruth was a policewoman in her mid-thirties. Her job required calm nerves and a level head, and she performed admirably. Nonetheless, when she went home at night she suffered from nightmares, rage, and anxiety. Many law enforcers might have similar reactions, and it might be plausible to say that this was a case of job-related stress. However, when Ruth came to see me, she regressed to a lifetime in which she had been a pale woman in Normandy wearing a white bonnet. She had been imprisoned unfairly in an unidentified building.

In that lifetime, Ruth had apparently been passive in accepting her confinement. She had never released her anger or corrected the wrongs that had put her there. She realized that this was a lesson she needed to learn in her current lifetime. As a policewoman, she has a strong sense of justice, a personality trait that was probably influenced by the past life experience. However, that experience also seemed to have left her with residual anger that was keeping her from being happy. In one sense Ruth seemed to be compensating for the experiences of the other lifetime in a healthy way, but in another she seemed to be overcompensating, to be clenching her teeth and saying, "No way am I ever going to let that happen again."

Sometimes, a cause-and-effect message such as this one is the point of a regression session. There may be a particular piece of information that needs to be learned, and once the patient learns it, he or she is able to assimilate it, grow, and simply go on. Ruth's memory helped her discern why she was so angry. It also helped her understand that the theme of her nightmares, which usually had to do with being trapped, confined, or paralyzed, was probably related to her imprisonment.

Ruth's nightmares have now disappeared, and her anxiety has lessened, although she still experiences anger at times. Whenever she begins to feel that rage, however, she is now able to control it much more quickly, and she is less frightened by it. Past life therapy helped her to clear two shadows in her life, and to lessen, control, and manage the one that remains.

Alice is a twenty-seven-year-old woman who suffered from anxiety and inability to trust, two very common symptoms in our society. Her symptoms had started in childhood. After her father locked her in a closet one day, severely frightening her, she had never again trusted her parents.

In regression, Alice returned to ancient times, to relate that she was a small child buried alive. Alice had fallen ill from a plague that had swept through her village. She had become feverish and was probably unconscious or even in a coma when she was mistaken for dead. She awakened in the grave and panicked. She was furious as she left that lifetime, realizing only later that the mistake had been an honest one. In life review, Alice was able to link that experience with lack of trust in this life.

Alice had a second past life memory of panicking as a child, this time during a war. People had collapsed on her during a bombardment, triggering symptoms of claustrophobia and extreme anxiety. After these two memories were accessed, Alice's symptoms began to dissipate. Understanding helped her symptoms, as it had also helped the musician, Tricia, and Ruth.

Revealing the source of a fear may not only alleviate that fear, it can also reveal talents from other lifetimes.

A young single mother and successful professional photographer named Caryn came to therapy to explore a number of relationship issues with family members. She was having some success in this arena with past life therapy. In addition, Caryn had another, very specific, problem. It was an uncharacteristic one for such a successful and independent woman. Caryn was terrified of getting lost while driving. To her dismay, she often did lose her way, perhaps more than the average person. At times, Caryn became so scared of this happening that she had to have someone drive her to appointments.

We decided to also address this fear with past life regression therapy. In hypnosis, Caryn recalled having been a navigator on a submarine during World War II. During one mission, she had become confused, had made a mistake and taken the ship way off course. The ship was so far off course that it had become lost in enemy waters. Detected by the enemy, the ship was destroyed, and Caryn and the other crew members were killed.

After this session, Caryn's fear of getting lost vanished completely.

Later, her young daughter observed how much better her mother had become, how much more loving.

After several months, Caryn dropped me a note. Even though she had been successful and functioned well prior to therapy, she described how "whole and full of love" she now felt and how at peace with herself she had become. She also reported that not only doesn't she get lost any more, but other people are asking *her* for instructions, and she draws maps for *them* so *they* don't lose their way!

Not only was Caryn able to overcome her fear, but she was also able to access her navigational talent from her previous lifetime and add it to her many others.

Past life regression sometimes gives great joy to adopted families by showing them that, although they are not biologically related and although blood *may* be thicker than water, spirit is thicker than blood. I have done regressions that indicate that the bonds between adopted children and their adoptive parents may be stronger than the bonds between these children and their biological parents. When various members of these adoptive families are regressed, they often recognize each other in prior lifetimes.

Experience has shown me that if a parent-child relationship is destined to take place, and the physical outlet is blocked, another way is found for it to occur. Parent-child relationships are never random. A friend of mine, an astrologer, has discovered the same thing. She has told me that if you compare the charts of adopted parents and children, you often see the same correspondences and connections that are seen in the charts of biological families.

Sometimes past life regression is the beginning of a spiritual path that brings not only understanding and special talents to consciousness but also peace, bliss, inner joy, and wisdom to the most mundane and unexpected moments of life. As an unforeseen result of past life therapy, many of my patients have become oriented toward spirituality or metaphysics without withdrawing, in any way, from productive careers and existing relationships. In fact, the other aspects of their lives have also improved and strengthened as a result of their spiritual growth. Many of them report more "peak" or transcendent experiences, more intuitive knowledge that leads them to betterment of both their inner and outer lives, and more peace, calm, and centeredness in their lives no matter the circumstances.

I know what they mean. As a result of my own spiritual growth, which in many ways began with my experiences with Catherine, I have had my own personal transcendent experiences. After the first one, I knew immediately that this state is a goal in itself.

The first one actually began about a week prior to the experience itself. Several years ago, after a ten-hour day of seeing patients, I was beginning to relax by meditating in a reclining chair in my office. After only a few minutes, already in a deep state without any particular thoughts in my mind, I heard a booming voice inside my head. It was like a telepathic trumpet, and it shook my whole body.

"Just love him!" the voice thundered. I was instantly wide awake. I knew the message meant Jordan, my son. At this time, he was a typically rebellious teenager, but I had not been thinking about him at all on this day. Perhaps, subconsciously, I was wrestling with how to deal with his behavior.

One very early and dark morning a week later, I was driving Jordan to school. I tried to get a conversation going, but he was particularly monosyllabic in his responses to me that day. Jordan was just plain grumpy.

I knew I had the choice of being angry or of letting it go. I remembered the message "Just love him!" and I chose the latter.

"Jordan, just remember that I love you," I said as I dropped him off at school.

To my surprise, he replied, "I love you, too."

It was then that I realized that he hadn't been angry or grumpy at all, he just wasn't fully awake yet. My perception of anger had been an illusion.

I continued driving in to the hospital, about forty-five minutes away. As I passed a church, the sun was just rising above the treetops, and a gardener was leisurely mowing the grass.

Suddenly I had a feeling of great peace and joy. I felt immensely safe and secure, and the world seemed to be in perfect order. The gardener, the trees, and everything else I could see were luminous and glowing. I could almost see through them; everything had a transparent golden quality. I felt connected to everyone and everything—to the gardener, the trees, the grass, the sky, a squirrel climbing a tree. There was the total absence of fear or anxiety. The future seemed perfectly clear . . . perfect.

I must have seemed strange to the other rush-hour commuters. I felt a kind of detached, universal love for them, too. Even as other drivers cut in front of me, I just waved them in and smiled. I wondered why all these people were rushing so much. Time seemed to stand still and then to disappear. I felt incredibly patient. We were here to learn and to love, I could see this so clearly. Nothing else really matters.

The luminosity and transparency of objects continued as I drove to the hospital. So did the state of detached loving-kindness and great peace and joy. So did the feelings of patience and happiness and interconnectedness with everything else.

This state stayed with me as I began my workday. I was unusually intuitive with my patients that morning, especially with two new patients I had never seen before. I could perceive light in and around people: everyone seemed to glow. I could really experience how everything in life is connected. I knew with certainty that there was no such thing as danger, no need for fear. Everything was one.

This experience lasted until I attended an administrative meeting later in the day. The subject of the meeting—How to Increase Hospital Profits—angered me. I knew that I again had a choice: to leave the meeting and maintain my state, or to stay and tell the truth about how I felt about their ideas. To stay and talk about ethics and honesty, I would need my left-brain, logical faculties. Immediately there was a profound shift. I was back to my "normal self," analytical and "down to earth." Afterwards, I was unable to bring back the wonderful, peaceful state. It was gone, no matter how hard I tried to remember, recall, recreate.

I have had this beautiful experience five or six times since then. Each time, it has come unbidden. Meditation does not create this state. It cannot be forced. It is not the result of effort. It is almost a gift, a gift of grace.

When I relax into a feeling of love, without asking for anything in return, I can sense that the state is very close by.

I also try now to help other people reach these states of inner peace, joy, and bliss that are the result of the sort of path of personal growth that can begin with past life regression. It is so important. For me, it is really the goal of all my therapy. It is this state of inner peace that is so healing, so therapeutic.

There are times when it is not necessary or even recommended to begin this path with past life regression therapy. Sometimes, hypnosis reveals a different path to be taken.

Occasionally a highly functioning, happy person comes to my office because of curiosity or "just for the experience." Often, such a patient has excellent results like Martha in Chapter Eight who was able to resolve the remaining grief she felt about her father's death as a result of her curiosity-motivated session. But sometimes these patients are not "successful."

Frequently, there is a reason memories are not forthcoming. Sometimes, these patients are trying *too* hard. The very act of trying is a conscious behavior that can block the subconscious from coming through. This block is easily overcome, however, as the patient relaxes and becomes more skilled at being passively receptive. Sometimes there is a fear of reliving a death experience. As discussed previously, I point out to my patients that they can choose whether to go through a death experience or not and that if they do, the majority of people do not find the death experience traumatic. This makes the success rate even higher.

But there are times when the patient has something more important to accomplish.

Armando is a tax attorney from New Jersey who came to see me for past life regression. He is an elegant man, impeccably dressed and charming, his mind ever attentive and quick. He was not having any significant psychological or physical problems, but he desperately wanted the experience of a past life regression. Armando was very serious about seeking spiritual growth.

Armando's personality style bordered on the obsessive-compulsive. He had difficulty relaxing and preferred spending leisure time alone or with his wife rather than with other people. Although always polite and considerate, he was not overly giving or charitable toward others. Politically, he was conservative and somewhat of a "hawk." As a student, he had abandoned his musical interests and talents for a more practical career in law.

During our second session, I hypnotized Armando to a deep level. He experienced an ecstatic state, filled with peace and love. He saw vivid colors, particularly purple, a deeply divine and holy color, a color traditionally associated with spirituality. But he could not retrieve any memories at all of past life experiences, although he was trying very hard.

I gave Armando a regression tape to play at home. His wife, whom I had not met, also listened to the tape. She had vivid visualizations of several past life scenes, and she recounted them to her envious husband. But Armando saw nothing of his previous lifetimes. Over the week between sessions, Armando's wife continued to have past life recall whenever she listened to the guided regression on the tape. Armando had none.

However, on the same tape I instruct the listener to meet a wise person, a guide or helper, to ask a question or two of this person, and to listen for the answer.

Out of Armando's purple light, his guide materialized. Armando's wise helper was a nineteen-year-old male with long blond hair, wearing blue jeans and a lumberjacket shirt. His name was Michael. The age, style, characteristics, and dress of his guide were not those one would expect a formal person like Armando to conjure up or imagine. Even Armando was surprised.

Michael was smiling. He put his arm around Armando and told him to "lighten up, relax, don't be so serious."

Whenever Armando listened to the tape, Michael would emerge out of this purple light and talk to him. He imparted spiritual advice, helped with practical wisdom regarding Armando's business and personal relationships, and made several accurate predictions of events that actually occurred over the next few days.

But Armando still desperately wanted a past life regression. He partially minimized the beauty and importance of the encounters with Michael, his guide.

Armando came in for his third session, still complaining that he could not recall his past lives. He envied his wife's easy recollections.

I hypnotized Armando to a deep level and had him find Michael.

"Ask *him* why you cannot remember your past lifetimes," I instructed.

Michael's answer was swift and to the point, as usual.

"You will be allowed to remember your lifetimes as a reward

when you give up your present fears. There is nothing to fear. You are afraid of people, and you should not be. Do not worry about others; they will be all right. Do not expect them to be perfect. Go to them to help them, even if you begin with just one at a time."

Armando did not really need to remember other lifetimes. His work is to be done in the present. Someday, if he is able to follow Michael's advice, he will be able to glimpse his past. But that glimpse will be a reward, a just desert.

The remembering of one's prior lifetimes is not essential or necessary for everyone. Not everyone has carried over blocks or scars that are significant in the current lifetime. Frequently, the emphasis is to be placed on the present, not the past. In his desire to remember his past lives, Armando nearly missed the incredibly beautiful and important meetings with Michael.

Armando's experience also begins to demonstrate the unlimited potential and resources of the subconscious mind in the hypnotic state. In this relaxed, peaceful state all kinds of things can happen. In a sense, when I conduct a regression I feel like a facilitator, a helper. It is the patient who ultimately controls the healing. Many different types of altered states, psychic insights, perception of beautiful colors, feelings, thoughts, and solutions to present problems may pop into the mind of a patient under regression, as well as experiences with guides and memories of past and present lifetimes. A patient may even have experiences that seem to take place in other realms altogether, realms that are very beautiful and sacred.

To see the answers to one's problems emblazoned in golden letters across a violet light is healing. An expansion of consciousness such as this is very therapeutic, a wonderful thing, and can be just as healing as past life regression.

The healing potential of the subconscious mind under the guidance of a good adviser or under one's own guidance seems limitless. I learn as much about healing from my patients as they do from their experiences, if not more. We are all teachers and students; we are all patients and healers. The journey through time into the mind, soul, and feelings is one that we all share.

11

The Techniques of Regression

IT IS NOT ALWAYS NECESSARY OR SOMETIMES EVEN POSsible to visit a past life regression therapist. I even recommend that my patients and those who attend my regression workshops augment their therapy or group experiences with techniques that can be used at home. You can use the same techniques to explore your own past lives and access your own higher wisdom. My patients tell me that the techniques described here have given them many kinds of stimulating, relaxing, and healing experiences.

A script for a version of a tape-recorded relaxation and regression meditation I give to patients and instructions on how to make your own tape appear in Appendix A. This exercise will guide your subconscious mind to uncover the most pertinent childhood, past life, or perhaps in-between-life memory for you to experience. The more often you use it, the more results you will get.

This script is similar to what I do in my office, but there are other very valuable techniques to a past life regression. These techniques appear in this chapter, and I recommend that you sample all of them to see which ones are the best and most enjoyable for you, and that you practice them regularly.

The other techniques that I recommend fall into four categories. They include keeping a dream journal, meditation and visualization, self-awareness techniques, and "play" techniques that you can try alone or with a friend. All will help you relax and focus your mind, allowing subconscious information to surface.

All of these techniques are safe. If you have a severe symptom or are anxious about the experience, you may want to begin your exploration by first consulting a trained therapist. Honor these feelings if you have them, but remember that the subconscious is very wise. It will usually give the experience appropriate for the moment and circumstances in which you find yourself. Even some of my patients with very disturbing symptoms have successfully used regression techniques at home between sessions.

However, the therapeutic process is very helpful in its ability to integrate an important past life experience into your present stage of growth. Therefore, if you ever have an experience you feel warrants help in order to integrate it into your present life situation, you may want to consult a professional therapist.

Explore, trust, play, and above all, be flexible. Allow yourself to be surprised at the directions in which your higher wisdom takes you as you begin to tap the many layers of your mind, body, emotions, and soul.

USING DREAMS FOR PAST LIFE RECALL

Start to keep a dream journal. Dreams often contain clues about past lives. Not all dreams are Freudian dreams with symbols, distortions, and wish-metaphors. Some dreams convey literal past life memories.

I have found the following method to be the best way to keep a dream journal. Upon awakening from sleep, lie quietly and try not to move. Try to remember your dream. Go over it in your mind. Then, go over it again, and more details will emerge.

Next, give your dream a title, such as "Paralyzed with Fear and Running without Moving" or "Being Lost in Labyrinths of German Castle." Giving the dream a title will help to identify its theme and will enable you to organize by category for subsequent retrieval. Writing down all of the dream's details will insure against the inevitable forgetting of the dream's content. Journal writing will also stimulate your mind to have better recall of your dreams and their details.

The more dreams you record, the more clues about your past lives you may receive. You can recognize a dream that holds a clue from a past life when you find you have dreamed you were dressed in clothing from a different period of time or when you are using tools or other implements that seem to date from a different place or time. For example, if you dream that you are dressed in the style of the American Revolution, or that you are repairing ancient Native American cliff dwellings, or that you are making candles from tallow, the odds are that your dream contains a clue to a past life.

You don't need to determine immediately the meaning of the clue. Simply write a narrative, give the dream a name, and occasionally review the contents of your entire journal for trends or patterns.

Do the details seem interrelated or random? Details of other places and times that can be integrated into a theme or picture may be giving you indications of the most important or relevant past lives for exploration, while the more random ones may be just that, random details, or else memory fragments that are not yet organized.

When you would like to more fully explore a past life detail or theme, meditate on it. Focus your mind on it as if you were doing a self-regression. Visualize that scene, image, or fragment and let it expand and move and become more detailed. Try not to inhibit your impressions mentally. Do not censor them. A fairly complete past life memory might evolve from a single meditation, or over several, or not at all. This is a natural variation. In the beginning it is common to receive a collection of past life fragments that do not seem coherent. The more you practice this technique, the more skilled you will become.

In my office, I sometimes ask a patient to play the parts of all the people in his or her dream. You can adapt this technique to use by yourself. For example, if you have a past life dream where you are surrounded by an unfamiliar family, imagine and perhaps enact the roles of the father, the mother, the younger sister, the boyfriend, etc. What does it feel like to be each of them?

Frequently, by using their intuition and imagination to play different roles and parts, people start to understand more about what their dreams really mean. They learn more about the motivations of each character. In past life dreams and also when working with actual regression material, playing each role in this manner may uncover a strong identification with a particular character.

Or, if you already identify with a particular character, the technique may allow you to empathize with the motivations of other people in the dream. You may come to recognize that one of the other characters in the dream is someone now in your present life. For instance, you might say, "This person feels just like my father."

In using this role-playing technique to interpret your more typical dreams, you may be able to find the patterns reflected in your present life.

USING MEDITATION AND VISUALIZATION FOR PAST LIFE RECALL

Meditation, a practice I recommend highly, is another basic method for opening up your awareness of past life memories. Meditation clears the mind, and when the mind is clear, insights, perceptions, and perhaps past life memories may spontaneously surface.

However, I also recommend meditation for its many other positive and far-reaching effects. Like keeping a dream journal, meditation is a technique that gives you a foundation of self-awareness that can be useful in many areas of your life. It teaches peacefulness and joy. It shows how to focus on the present moment and not to worry so much about the future or ruminate about the past. It can teach you to be in control of your mind and emotions instead of the other way around.

The practice of meditation is much easier and simpler than most people believe it to be. The beginner's anxiety about doing it correctly, the *right* way, is what creates the difficulty. However, there is no one right way to meditate. Whenever you are relaxed, when your mind is quiet and observant, when you are not reflexively engaged in thought, you are meditating. You could be sitting cross-legged on the floor with your back straight, or in a chair, or lying down, or in any other comfortable position. Whatever position you're in, the observant, aware, quiet mind is a meditating mind.

In meditation there is an active awareness, a state of open receptivity, an observing consciousness that breaks down the barriers between the observer and the observed object. Great insights and revelations can occur in this state. Meditation takes practice and patience, but the very act of meditating creates more patience.

As a psychiatrist, I know how difficult it can be to quiet the mind. Thoughts always seem to be popping up into our consciousness. As a matter of fact, most of us are not even aware of these thoughts or that we are constantly thinking, visualizing, or daydreaming. In my workshops I ask people to close their eyes and think of nothing for thirty seconds—no thoughts, no images, just a blank mind.

Almost no one can do this. After the thirty seconds are up, I ask people to tell me whether they had any thoughts, and, if so, what they were. "Why is he asking us to do this?" "This is silly." "My back hurts." "I wonder if I left my headlights on." "I wish that person would stop coughing." These are examples of the constant inner chatter that floods the minds of my workshop participants. Try it for yourself and see.

To meditate, find a quiet, peaceful place and just relax and try to quiet your mind. Pay attention to your breathing. Breathe slowly and gently, slowly and gently, until your breathing settles into a calm, even rhythm. Become aware of your thoughts and then softly let them go. Do not judge yourself. Do not become frustrated or impatient. Just observe your thoughts as they pass by.

As you do so you will learn a great deal about yourself, and as you practice the techniques in this chapter and in Appendix A, you may access a past life memory. With time, meditating may enhance your success with other techniques of regression.

Some people prefer to meditate by concentrating on a word, a number, or an object. Again, the specific technique does not matter. As your mind and body relax, the brain's electrical activity slows, and you enter an alpha or even a theta state, states in which the electrical wave activity of the brain decreases to a much slower rhythm than that of the normal waking, or beta, state.

When you are in these relaxed states, you are meditating; you are restoring yourself; you are rejuvenating. Other people prefer visualizing, or picturing things in their mind's eye as a meditation technique. This is very similar to daydreaming. But when I measure the electrical activity of the brain in people who are meditating and people who are visualizing, I find the same alpha and theta states. Those who visualize are also meditating, but in a more guided way.

Visualization can be used as a powerful healing technique to augment the body's immune system, accelerate natural homeostatic and healing mechanisms, and eliminate many types of illnesses. It can also be used to enhance a physical performance, as a form of prayer, or even to reach transcendent states.

To discover a past life from a meditative state, visualize yourself in a different time. Let the images flow into your conscious mind. The material that comes up will be arising from your deeper mind, your subconscious. Don't analyze the images. Just let them flow forth and observe them as if you were a witness to the events or scenes they portray. Use your imagination. After you are finished, record your experiences in a journal, perhaps in a separate section of your dream journal. Look for patterns and meanings the same way you do when you examine your dreams.

If you'd like more information about different meditation techniques, consult some of the books on the Suggested Reading List in Appendix B. Many different types of meditation tapes are also available.

SELF-OBSERVATION AS A KEY TO PAST LIFE RECALL

Your current life and circumstances often contain clues to your past lives. So, when you're relaxed and have some free time, try some self-analysis. From a detached, nonjudgmental, and uncritical perspective, observe and ruminate upon your talents and abilities. Where do they come from? Did you inherit them from your parents, or could they be connected to a past life?

A classic example of a talent potentially inherited from a past life is Mozart's ability to write symphonies at the age of five. It could easily be hypothesized that Mozart might have been a musician in prior lifetimes, improved upon his talents, and brought them over to his current lifetime.

A facility for a particular language or an affinity for a certain culture may also be a clue to past life origins. For example, in a lecture of mine I met a Caucasian man from Oklahoma who spends all of his vacations in Jamaica. He loves the people and the culture and understands it as well as a native. What's more, he felt "at home" upon arriving there for the first time. You can use your current talents as a focus for accessing past lives through hypnotic regression techniques or through visualization.

The remnants of negative experiences you had during other lifetimes might have surfaced as fears or phobias in this lifetime. Take an inventory of yourself. Become aware of any fears or phobias you have. Ask yourself, Where does the fear come from? Why do I have it? Did something happen to me as a child to cause it? Did I always have that fear?

If you can't find a source for the fear, and you realize that it is one you have always had, start playing, dreaming, and visualizing, and you might find the source in a past lifetime.

It's important to stress that to be successful in this exercise, as in all the others, you need to be nonjudgmental and uncritical. For instance, if you address a fear of water by saying, "Oh, I'm just afraid of water; I'm a coward and that's all there is to it," you'll never find a possible past life connection to a drowning.

Although some people find an affinity to a certain culture, others are repulsed by certain areas of the world. A housewife and mother of three recalled having a severe panic attack when her plane landed at Athens Airport for the start of her honeymoon. She insisted that she and her husband leave Greece at once. They flew to Rome and later to Paris with no recurrence of the terrifying symptoms, and they had a wonderful time.

In a regression session years later, this woman remembered a Greek lifetime when she was pushed off a cliff to her death by people who had violently disagreed with her beliefs. Critics might argue that this woman's panic upon landing in Greece was the result of repressed fears about her new marriage. But the complete disappearance of the symptoms when they arrived in another country refutes such an argument.

Others uncover clues about past lives through experiences of déjà vu. Have you ever had a strange feeling of "having been there before" when first visiting a place? After one of my lectures, a couple in their early fifties told me about a recent trip to Italy. This was their first trip to this country, where neither one understood or spoke the language. The couple rented a car and lost their way while driving through northern Italy. Becoming increasingly anxious as nightfall approached, they entered a small town.

The wife suddenly had a strange feeling of déjà vu. The town seemed hauntingly familiar to her. Her husband described the glazed look that came over her eyes at the moment. He was shocked when she began speaking Italian to the villagers, who assumed that she knew their language. In fact, she had never studied or spoken Italian in her life. Not in *this* life.

Have you ever had a spontaneous reverie of being in a different place, different time, different body? This might not be just a daydream. Children frequently report such reveries, which might be past life memories. But many adults do, too.

Have you ever noticed a particular, unexplainable attraction to someone or a puzzling dislike for another person? You might have been together before.

Observe your likes and dislikes, your clothes, and your habits. What are your dominant personality traits? Look around your home. What art and furniture motifs are present? What decorative styles? Keep a clear, calm, and open mind as you look around. One patient of mine couldn't come up with any pattern to her collections. She denied having an affinity or attraction to any particular historical period or culture. It fell to the friend who had accompanied her to the session to point out that the patient's entire home was filled with nineteenth-century Japanese art! So relax and do not neglect to see what might be looming all around you.

Don't worry about whether or not this information is "real." Your mind is producing this material, and the exercise will have the same effect as dreams. That is, this process will stimulate your mind to render more and more valid past life material. Your aim, initially, is to open doorways and establish pathways. Later on, with experience, you can be more analytical. You'll know when that time has come.

"PLAY" TECHNIQUES FOR ACCESSING YOUR PAST LIVES

Free-associating with emotionally charged words and phrases might help you access your past lives. There are certain universal words that transcend cultures and lifetimes; they are fixtures throughout the ages. A partial list of them, adapted from Gloria Chadwick's *Discovering Your Past Lives*, appears below. Feel free to add your own words and phrases to the list.

When you are relaxed, close your eyes and think or say one of these words. Then observe the mental images, scenes, and feelings that result. Or, tape record the list and play back the tape. Take your time, lingering with each word as the scenes and feelings arise and flow across your mind.

War	*Church*
Peace	*Spear*
Desert	*Ocean*
Soldiers Marching	*Mountain*

Ships *Cave*
Gun *Sunset*
Knives *Pain*
Mob *Music*
Hanging *Officer*
Execution *Horse*
Hunger *Animal*
Starving *Flood*
Slave *Poison*
King *Healer*
Book *Medicine Man*
Pen Writing *Body*
Night Sky *Funeral*
Stars *Birth*

Afterward, write down the images in your journal. Use them later to look for past life patterns or themes, or use them as clues for your regression and visualization sessions. For example, if you free-associated with the word *soldier* and then saw yourself marching in the Civil War, you might write the image down in your journal and then meditate upon it the next day, week, or even months later. It helps to be open and playful when trying this exercise.

As an aside, past lives during the Civil War are very common. Many people have a déjà vu experience when visiting Civil War graves and battle sites.

The technique I call "Faces" is another "play" method to remember past lives. Sit a few feet across from a friend, with the lights dim and with soft music in the background. Look into the other person's face. Watch to see if the person's face changes. Observe and describe the changes you see. Features often do appear to change. Eyes, noses, and hairstyles dissolve and re-form. Headgear sometimes appears.

You can also try this exercise alone, by using a mirror and observing the changes you see in your own face.

If you notice a white light extending one to several inches from your friend's head or even your own mirrored reflection, you might be seeing a manifestation of the energy field extending outward beyond the physical body. Many people report seeing this "aura," which sometimes appears in colors. I have studied several people who have independently described the very same pattern of colors in the aura of another person. When I had them watch or "read" another person's energy field, their descriptions were also identical to each other.

I first tried this exercise with several people in my office, and they were able to see the transformations in facial features, in skin color, hair, eyes, and so on. Still, I worried that this simple approach might seem silly or foolish, or just be perceptual distortion, and I was reluctant to introduce it as an exercise in my workshops. Finally, near the end of an exciting workshop with a cooperative group of several hundred people, I decided to take the plunge.

Over one hundred pairs of workshop participants sat facing each other in a dimly lit hotel ballroom, gazing into each other's faces. After a period of time, people were instructed to find a new partner and again try the exercise. The results surprised us all. The majority of people saw their partners' faces change dramatically into a series of faces, some very ancient-looking. Some people had psychic experiences, in which they saw faces that they later discovered resembled their partner's dead relatives. Others saw features that looked as though they belonged to spiritual guides. Still others saw the faces of figures their partners have seen only in past life regression, or that psychics had described to them.

When we changed partners, oftentimes the same faces were observed in the very same people by their new partners. Many people saw auras for the first time. One fourteen-year-old boy was able to psychically pick up information about his partners. He had never done this before. Since then, I have included Faces in every workshop. The results are consistently dramatic, and it's a lot of fun. The only secret to Faces is to make sure you try it in a dimly lit room. This frees up the left brain and allows easier passage of intuitive impressions.

Faces can provide clues to many different past lives. As in other methods, meditation, visualization, and/or free association to the observed changes can fill out the memory. Let them expand and develop, without censoring the material. A face may become a group of faces, or a whole scene may unfold behind the face. You may hear a voice or an important word. Try it and see.

Visiting a reputable psychic who can also do past life readings is another interesting recall technique that can be very enjoyable. The psychic might be able to provide you with valuable clues, or you might feel something resonate within you as he or she speaks. Memories might even be triggered. A psychic reading is not as emotionally charged as a regression session, when your own memory bank is stirred, and your own images and feelings flood your awareness. As a result, therapeutic change does not occur. Yet, a session with a good psychic can be an enjoyable experience and might provide some thought-provoking clues to your past.

Beatrice Rich, a well-known psychic in New York and Miami, told me about a client who wanted more than the usual psychic reading. This man, a business executive, wanted a past life reading, too. Working with psychometry, which is the art of receiving psychic impressions from holding an object belonging to the client, Beatrice saw this man's body change. His arms became darker, much thicker, and more muscular. She saw that he was a soldier and a skilled archer. Unbeknownst to her, the man, who lived in New York City, had one passion above all others—archery. Had she psychically picked up on his interest? Was she reading his mind and elaborating a scenario? Or was she actually viewing a scene from one of his past lives, a life that was also pertinent to this man's present?

While Beatrice was reading another client, the room became hazy to her and she saw the woman transformed into a Turkish lady who had sold bracelets and trinkets in a bazaar hundreds of years ago. Afterwards, the client removed her jacket and rolled up the sleeve of her blouse to reveal an arm covered with bracelets. They both laughed. Was Beatrice's vision just a psychic impression of her client's wardrobe? Or was it an actual scene from a past life? Even Beatrice is not sure.

On another occasion, she kept seeing a woman change from an ancient Hawaiian to someone from an old Northern European culture, back to her current body, and then the cycle began over again. This client repeatedly vacations in only two places, Hawaii and Scandinavia.

Beatrice saw another client, a college student, in a different body living in a primitive culture thousands of years ago. She described an ancient spoonlike device with which this man was able to sling objects, such as crude arrows or darts. She described the long row of huts along the riverbank and the fierce warrior tribes who lived upriver. This student's archeology professor claimed no such weapon had ever existed, but the client finally found a picture of it in a textbook. Beatrice had never seen this weapon before she had her psychic vision.

Another method for triggering past life recall is body work. Some memories appear to be connected to actual areas of the physical body, a sort of cellular memory. Many people undergoing acupressure massage, kinesiology, reflexology, and other methods of stimulating key areas of the physical body experience flashes of past life scenes. A person who in a former life was lanced in the lower back, for example, might reexperience this traumatic event during a vigorous massage stimulation at the identical site in the current body. Sometimes the trigger site is in a different place, often in the lower legs and feet.

The experience I had during acupressure massages, described earlier, is a good example of this phenomenon. During one session while the acupressure therapist worked on my feet, I had reached a very deep state of relaxation. Suddenly, I began to have a vivid and detailed memory of having been a priest in the ancient Near East!

If you have such a memory, or even a fragment of a memory, write it down in your journal. Later on, you may see that it is part of a larger pattern, or you might be able to elaborate on it with the techniques described here.

A final but important point. Do not be surprised if these techniques or the regression exercise in the next chapter lead you to a place that is not a past life. When I regress patients, I do not know where their higher wisdom will take us. Often the destination is a past life or series of past lives. But sometimes that destination is childhood, or a healing garden, or the mystical, light-filled place that seems to exist between lives. In every case, it will be your subconscious wisdom that decides the best place for you. Often, when conducting a regression, I feel as though I am only along for the ride.

You may also experience new places and experiences when you use these techniques, perhaps even places and experiences that are not described in this book and where I have never been. Allow yourself the possibility of being surprised by an unexpected experience. Often, these are the ones that induce the most growth.

Instead of experiencing a past life, you may go to a place and read the mystical records, like Beth did in Chapter Nine. You may meet a loved one in a garden who gives just one sentence of advice, as Betsy's father gave her in Chapter Five. You may even experience other realities, other dimensions, beyond the traditional reference points of space and time.

Let your growth evolve in an intuitive, nonlinear way if that is the pattern that it takes. As long as you allow yourself to feel playful and nonjudgmental about your experiences, you will always continue to grow.

Remember, if something comes up that really troubles you, you can go to a therapist to resolve it. Most people, however, remember experiences, whether from childhood or a past life or elsewhere, without significant discomfort or anxiety. I have regressed many people in large groups and have never had any problems. You will never get "stuck" in the places where you go. You always have the option of opening your eyes or floating above your experience. You have the choice. Your subconscious mind is always in control; it is not going to allow something to happen that you cannot handle.

Finally, these techniques for recalling your past lives, or, at least, for being able to become aware of some of the clues and signposts along the way, are by no means the only ones. Studies have been done of past life recall that occurs during electrical stimulation of certain areas of the brain, of memories retrieved while on drugs or in altered mental states, from comas, near death and out-of-body experiences, and in many other ways. There is excitement in this exploration and study. There is an exhilaration when you realize how much greater you are than your current, confined ego or personality. The real you, the immortal you, is the you that is present from body to body, from life to life. How exciting it is to meet yourself!

Appendix A
MAKING YOUR OWN RELAXATION AND REGRESSION TAPE

THE FOLLOWING IS A WRITTEN VERSION OF THE RELAXATION and regression tape I supply to my own patients and to workshop participants so that they can continue the regression process at home. Some of the patients whose stories appear in this book have used this exercise with excellent results.

You can use this tape to have an actual regression, or to relax and become peaceful and get in touch with your personal wisdom.

Remember once again that you may have a very vivid and complete regression experience right away, or you may experience the key moment flow pattern, or you may begin with only fragments or images of past life or between-life experiences. You may find yourself in a garden, or a temple, or in another healing or spiritual space, or you may simply feel relaxation and a sense of well-being. Let any of these experiences be the right one for you at the time. Allow yourself to be surprised by the unexpected if it happens. And keep in mind that the more you practice this process, the easier it gets and the more rewards you will have.

The tape method does not work for everyone. Some people need to listen to the tape several times before they experience its benefits. An inability to respond to the tape does not mean that the person cannot be regressed. It might mean that the "nonresponder" needs the individual attention and direction of a therapist.

The script is intended only as a guide, as an example, and you should tape it and use it only if you feel comfortable trying to go back to retrieve memories from your past, as some memories may be disturbing to you. If you are concerned about the effects of a traumatic memory, do not make the tape. Or, you might want to tape only the relaxation portion of the exercise, since this is quite valuable in itself.

As I have previously discussed, the risks of a disturbing reaction are minimal. Most people handle and integrate the memories without difficulty. They actually feel much better. The tape technique is powerful, though. If you make one and use it by yourself, there is a risk, even if only slight, of an adverse effect, such as anxiety or guilt. If this happens, you should then see a therapist and resolve any problems that might have occurred.

As you make the tape, read the script in a calm and slow voice, pausing slightly when you come to an ellipsis (. . .) and pausing for a longer time when the direction to pause is in brackets. (Note: Read the directions in brackets to yourself, not out loud.) Before you turn on your tape recorder, you may want to practice reading the script several times to find a rhythm that is comfortable for you and that allows enough time for you to respond to the instructions.

Do not hurry the recording process. There is no right or wrong amount of time for this exercise.

Play back the recording when you are in a quiet and private place where you can relax and at a time when you know you will not be disturbed.

DO NOT PLAY THIS TAPE IN A CAR.

Before you start the tape, lie down on a bed or sit in a comfortable chair and loosen any tight-fitting clothes. Make sure there will be no distractions or interruptions. Kick off your shoes; take off your glasses; take out your contact lenses. Allow yourself to relax completely. Do not cross your legs. You might want to play soft, gentle music in the background if music is soothing to you.

As an alternative to the tape, you can have a friend read the script to you.

SCRIPT FOR RELAXATION AND REGRESSION TAPE

Allow your eyes to close.

Now focus on your breathing, which should be deep and regular, from way down to way up.

Take five deep, relaxing breaths, breathing in through your nose and out through your mouth . . . relax [take a long pause for the five breaths].

Now with each exhaling, breathe out the aches and pains and tension stored in your body.

With each inhaling breath, breathe in the peaceful energy that surrounds you.

Relax even more deeply.

Now visualize or imagine or feel all of your muscles completely relaxing.

Relax the muscles of your forehead and your face . . .

And your jaw . . .

Relax the muscles of your neck and shoulders. A lot of tension is stored in these areas.

Relax your arms . . .

Relax your legs . . .

Relax your back muscles . . .

And allow the muscles of your stomach to relax completely, so that your breathing stays nice and deep and even.

With each gentle breath you take, allow yourself to become more and more deeply relaxed.

Visualize, imagine, or feel a bright light at the top of your head, inside your head. Allow your mind to choose the color of this light [pause].

Everything that this beautiful light touches, as it later spreads down your body, every tissue and organ and muscle, every fiber and cell of your body will relax completely, getting rid of all aches and pains, of all illness.

And the light will deepen and deepen the level of your relaxation.

You are already feeling deeply peaceful and tranquil.

Now see or feel or imagine the light spreading down from the top of your head . . . down past your forehead . . . behind your eyes . . . relaxing you even more.

You can see or feel or imagine the light spreading into your jaw . . . down your scalp . . . deepening your state.

Now the light is flowing into your neck, completely relaxing the muscles of the neck and throat, smoothing out the lining of your throat.
And you relax even more [pause].

Visualize, imagine, or feel the light, which relaxes and heals every muscle, nerve, and cell of your body, spreading into your shoulders . . .
And down both arms, all the way to your hands and your fingers [pause].

See or feel or imagine the light flowing into your upper back . . . and chest . . . and into your heart, which pumps the light through every blood vessel of your body . . .
Into your lungs, glowing beautifully . . .
The muscles of your upper back are completely relaxed.
And now the light is spreading into your spinal cord, from your brain to the tip of your spine, flowing along your entire nervous system to reach every muscle and cell of your body.
And you are deeply calm and relaxed.
You are feeling a deep tranquility, a marvelous sense of peace [pause].

See, imagine, or feel the light spreading into your abdomen . . . and your lower back, completely relaxing those muscles and nerves . . .
And now see it flowing into your hips . . .
Into your legs, and all the way to your feet and your toes, so that your entire body is filled . . . bathed . . . with the wonderful, bright light.
And you feel very, very peaceful.

Now visualize, imagine, or feel the light completely surrounding your body, as if you were in a cocoon or halo of light. This protects you and relaxes your skin and outer muscles . . .
And you feel even more peaceful, calm, and relaxed.

In a moment I am going to count backwards, from five to one. With each number, you will feel more and more peaceful and calm, and the level of your relaxed state will deepen and deepen, until by the time I reach one, you will be in a very deep state, your mind freed up beyond the normal limits of space and time.
You are able to remember everything.

Five . . .
Four, feeling more and more peaceful and relaxed . . .
Three, deeper and deeper and deeper . . .

Two, nearly there . . .
One . . .

You are in a deeply relaxed state, but if you feel any discomfort, now or later, you are in complete control.
You can now end the relaxation part of the exercise and not proceed with the regression merely by opening your eyes, and you will immediately return to your normal state, with full control of all your psychological and physical functions, feeling wonderful, relaxed, and refreshed.

If you choose to go further, visualize, imagine, or feel yourself slowly walking down a beautiful staircase [pause].
At the bottom, there is a doorway with a bright light on the other side.
You are feeling completely relaxed and very much at peace.
You walk toward the door, knowing that your mind is no longer limited by space or by time, and that you can remember everything that has ever happened to you.
When you pass through the door into the light, you will be in another time.
Allow your subconscious mind to choose the time, whether from this life or from any other.
You may be going back to a time from which a symptom of yours, a feeling, or a troubling relationship first arose, the root cause [long pause].

Emerging into the light, first look down at your feet. See what kind of footwear you are wearing, whether shoes or sandals or cloth or none at all . . .
Then begin to look up your body . . .
Look at your clothes . . .
Look at your hands . . .
See what you look like . . .
Is it daytime or nighttime . . .
Are you inside or outside . . .
See if you know or can find out the date [pause].
Look around, observing the geography, the architecture, the plants and trees, and whether other people are around. If there are other people, you can talk to them and they might answer your questions.
Find out the answers to your questions, to your symptoms [long pause].
Spend more time exploring that period.

You can go backward or forward in time if you need to . . .

If you feel any anxiety, just float above your body, observing rather than actively feeling and participating.
Or simply open your eyes and end the procedure, if you choose.

Explore any significant events and understand, from your greater perspective, why they happened and what they really mean.
You can understand now [long pause].

See if any people from that lifetime are with you in your current life [long pause].

If you wish, go to the end of that lifetime and experience your death [long pause].

Float above your body and review your life. What lessons did you have to learn? [long pause]

Now it is time to come back.
In a moment, I am going to count from one to five. At the count of five, open your eyes and you will be wide awake, alert and refreshed, feeling wonderful. You will be in full control of all your physical and psychological functions. You will remember everything. Every time you do this exercise, you will find that you will be more deeply and deeply relaxed.

One: *Every muscle and nerve of your body fully relaxed.*
Two: *Gradually awakening, feeling wonderful.*
Three: *More and more awake and alert.*
Four: *Nearly awake, feeling great.*
Five: *Open your eyes, wide awake and alert, feeling wonderful.*

Appendix B
SUGGESTED READING LIST

NEAR DEATH AND REINCARNATION

Jeanne Avery
Astrology and Your Past Lives
Richard Bach
One
Illusions
Henry L. Bolduc
The Journey Within: Past Life and Channeling
Gina Cerminara
Many Mansions: The Edgar Cayce Story on Reincarnation
Many Lives, Many Loves
World Within
Anabel Chaplin
The Bright Light of Death
Barbara Clow
Eye of the Centaur: A Visionary Guide into Past Lives
Sylvia Cranston and Carey Williams
Reincarnation: A New Horizon in Science, Religion, and Society
Adrian Finkelstein, M.D.
Your Past Lives and the Healing Process
Edith Fiore
You Have Been Here Before: A Psychologist Looks at Past Lives
Joe Fisher
The Case for Reincarnation
Bernard Gittelson and Laura Torbet
Intangible Evidence

Bruce Goldberg
Past Lives, Future Lives
Joan Grant
Far Memory
Winged Pharaoh
Elizabeth Haich
Initiation
Manley P. Hall
Reincarnation: The Cycles of Necessity
Past Lives and Present Problems
Virginia Hanson
Karma
Joseph Head and S. L. Cranston
Reincarnation: The Phoenix Fire Mystery
Irene Hickman
Mind Probe-Hypnosis
Jon Klimo
Channeling: Investigations on Receiving Information from Paranormal Sources
Noel Langley
Edgar Cayce on Reincarnation
Frederick Lenz
Lifetimes: True Accounts of Reincarnation
Geddes MacGregor
Reincarnation in Christianity
Ruth Montgomery
Here and Hereafter
Raymond A. Moody, Jr., M.D.
Life After Life
The Light Beyond
Melvin Morse, M.D., and Paul Perry
Closer to the Light: Learning from the Near-Death Experiences of Children
Kenneth Ring
Heading Toward Omega: In Search of the Meaning of the Near-Death Experience
Jane Roberts
The Seth Material
D. Scott Rogo
The Search for Yesterday: A Critical Examination of the Evidence of Reincarnation

Karl Schlotterbeck

Living Your Past Lives: The Psychology of Past Life Regression

Chet B. Snow and Helen Wambach

Mass Dreams of the Future: What Thousands of People Under Future Life Regression Have Revealed About the Coming Apocalyptic New Age

Lynn E. Sparrow

Edgar Cayce and the Born Again Christian

Jess Stearn

Edgar Cayce: The Sleeping Prophet

Soulmates

Brad Steiger and Francie Steiger

The Star People

Discover Your Past Lives

Rudolf Steiner

Reincarnation and Immortality

Ian Stevenson

Twenty Cases Suggestive of Reincarnation

Thomas Sugrue

There Is a River

Dick Sutphen and Lauren L. Taylor

Past Life Therapy in Action

John Van Auken

Past Lives, Present Relationships: How Karma Affects You and Your Relationships

Helen Wambach

Life Before Life

Brian L. Weiss, M.D.

Many Lives, Many Masters

Joel Whitton and Joe Fisher

Life Between Life: Scientific Explorations into the Void Separating One Incarnation from the Next

Mary Ann Woodward

Edgar Cayce's Story of Karma

Roger Woolger

Other Lives, Other Selves: A Jungian Psychotherapist Discovers Past Lives

HEALING AND ALTERNATIVE MEDICINE

Shepherd Bliss, editor
The New Holistic Health Handbook: Living Well in a New Age
Joan Borysenko, Ph.D.
Minding the Body, Mending the Mind
Barbara Ann Brennan
Hands of Light
Deepak Chopra, M.D.
Quantum Healing
Norman Cousins
Anatomy of an Illness as Perceived by the Patient
Stephen Cummings, F.N.P., and Dana Ullman, M.P.H.
Everybody's Guide to Homeopathic Medicines
Richard Gerber, M.D.
Vibrational Medicine: New Choices for Healing Ourselves
Louise L. Hay
You Can Heal Your Life
Dennis T. Jaffe, Ph.D.
Healing from Within
Gerald Jampolsky
Teach Only Love: The Seven Principles of Attitudinal Healing
W. Brugh Joy, M.D.
Joy's Way
Ted Kaptchuk and Michael Croucher
The Healing Arts: Exploring the Medical Ways of the World
Elisabeth Kübler-Ross
Death, the Final Stage of Growth
On Death and Dying
Stephen Levine
Who Dies
Richard Moss
The Black Butterfly: An Invitation to Radical Aliveness
How Shall I Live: Where Spiritual Healing and Conventional Medicine Meet
Bobbie Probstein
Return to Center
Bernard S. Siegel, M.D.
Love, Medicine and Miracles

Index

PIATKUS BOOKS

If you have enjoyed reading this book, you may be interested in other titles published by Piatkus. These include:

0 7499 2293 1	10 Steps to Psychic Power	Cassandra Eason	£12.99
0 7499 2459 4	5-Minute Meditator, The	Eric Harrison	£7.99
0 7499 2160 9	A Woman's Spiritual Journey	Joan Borysenko	£12.99
0 7499 1581 1	At Peace In The Light	Dannion Brinkley	£10.99
0 7499 2516 7	Babe Bible	Anita Naik	£9.99
0 7499 2110 2	Balancing Your Chakras	Sonia Choquette	£9.99
0 7499 1981 7	Barefoot Doctor's Handbook For Heroes	Barefoot Doctor	£9.99
0 7499 2201 X	Believing It All	Marc Parent	£9.99
0 7499 1969 8	Book Of Shadows	Phyllis Curott	£10.99
0 7499 2465 9	Celebrity Style Secrets	Jacqui Ripley	£7.99
0 7499 1168 9	Care Of The Soul	Thomas Moore	£10.99
0 7499 1763 6	Changes	Soozi Holbeche	£8.99
0 7499 1892 6	Channelling	Lita de Alberdi	£9.99
0 7499 1773 3	Children & The Spirit World	Linda Williamson	£8.99
0 7499 1929 9	Chinese Face and Hand Reading	J. O'Brien and M. Palmer	£8.99
0 7499 1824 1	Clear Your Clutter With Feng Shui	Karen Kingston	£7.99
0 7499 2049 1	Colour Healing Manual	Pauline Wills	£12.99
0 7499 1846 2	Colour Your Life	Howard and Dorothy Sun	£10.99
0 7499 2096 3	Colours of the Soul	June McLeod	£10.99
0 7499 2209 5	Complete Book of Women's Wisdom	Cassandra Eason	£10.99
0 7499 2079 3	Dolphin Healing	Horace Dobbs	£10.99
0 7499 2240 0	Encyclopedia of Magic and Ancient Wisdom	Cassandra Eason	£12.99
0 7499 2158 7	Endorphin Effect, The	William Bloom	£12.99
0 7499 2303 2	Energy Healing For Beginners	Ruth White	£9.99

ISBN	Title	Author	Price
0 7499 1868 3	Essential Nostradamus, The	Peter Lemesurier	£5.99
0 7499 2415 2	Everyday Karma	Carmen Harra	£9.99
0 7499 1927 2	Everyday Rituals and Ceromonies	Lorna St Aubyn	£8.99
0 7499 2143 9	Finding Fulfilment	Liz Simpson	£8.99
0 7499 2295 8	Heal Yourself	Anne Jones	£10.99
0 7499 1942 6	Healers and Healing	Roy Stemman	£8.99
0 7499 2308 3	Healing Journey, The	Matthew Manning	£12.99
0 7499 2491 8	Help Your Child Succeed at School	Hilary Wilce	£8.99
0 7499 2505 1	How to Clean Absolutely Everything	Barty Phillips	£7.99
0 7499 1265 0	I Ching Or Book Of Changes, The	Brian Browne Walker	£7.99
0 7499 2156 0	Jonathan Cainer's Guide To The Zodiac	Jonathan Cainer	£12.99
0 7499 1510 2	Journey of Self Discovery	Ambika Wauters	£8.99
0 7499 2441 1	Joy Diet, The	Martha Beck	£10.99
0 7499 2182 X	Life on the Other Side	Sylvia Browne	£12.99
0 7499 2247 8	Little Book of Women's Wisdom, The	Judy Ashberg	£4.99
0 7499 2497 7	Living Druidry	Emma Restall Orr	£10.99
0 7499 2071 8	Living Magically	Gill Edwards	£9.99
0 7499 2339 3	Make Your Dreams Come True	Ulli Springett	£9.99
0 7499 1378 9	Many Lives, Many Masters	Brian Weiss	£9.99
0 7499 1958 2	Meditation Plan, The	Richard Lawrence	£10.50
0 7499 2390 3	Modern Girl's Guide to Dynamic Dating	Sarah Ivens	£6.99
0 7499 2424 1	Modern Girl's Guide to Etiquette, A	Sarah Ivens	£6.99
0 7499 2268 0	Modern Girl's Guide to Getting Hitched, A	Sarah Ivens	£6.99
0 7499 1979 5	One Last Time	John Edward	£9.99
0 7499 2394 6	One-Liners	Ram Dass	£4.99
0 7499 1620 6	Only Love Is Real	Brian Weiss	£9.99

0 7499 2091 2	Other Side and Back, The	Sylvia Browne	£12.99
0 7499 2089 0	Palmistry in the 21st Century	Lori Reid	£8.99
0 7499 2228 1	Past Lives, Future Healing	Sylvia Browne	£12.99
0 7499 1377 0	Past Lives, Present Dreams	Denise Linn	£8.99
0 7499 2392 X	Peace Angels	Antoinette Sampson	£6.99
0 7499 2064 5	Pendulum Dowsing	Cassandra Eason	£7.99
0 7499 1948 5	Power of Inner Peace, The	Diana Cooper	£10.50
0 7499 2422 5	Power of Karma, The	Mary T. Browne	£7.99
0 7499 2024 6	Psychic World of Derek Acorah, The	Derek Acorah	£9.99
0 7499 2437 3	Queen Bees and Wannabes	Rosalind Wiseman	£7.99
0 7499 2120 X	Radionics Handbook, The	Keith Mason	£10.99
0 7499 1995 7	Reaching To Heaven	James Van Praagh	£9.99
0 7499 2338 5	Reading the Future	Sasha Fenton	£10.99
0 7499 2066 1	Reiki for Common Ailments	Mari Hall	£12.99
0 7499 2530 2	Reincarnation	Roy Stemman	£7.99
0 7499 1878 0	Right Way to Write	Rupert Morris	£9.99
0 7499 2233 8	Ruth the Truth's Psychic Guide	Ruth Urquhart	£8.99
0 7499 2196 X	Sacred Healing	Jack and Jan Angelo	£14.99
0 7499 1404 1	Saved By The Light	Dannion Brinkley	£9.99
0 7499 2375 X	Seven Steps to Heaven	Joyce Keller	£9.99
0 7499 1961 2	Soul Purpose	Jackee Holder	£12.99
0 7499 2072 6	Stepping Into The Magic	Gill Edwards	£9.99
0 7499 2321 0	Sylvia Browne's Book Of Dreams	Sylvia Browne	£10.99
0 7499 2246 X	Symbol Therapy	Ulli Springett	£8.99
0 7499 1009 7	Tarot Made Easy	Nancy Garen	£12.99
0 7499 2521 3	What Friends Are For	Megan Hess	£6.99
0 7499 2490 X	What Mothers Do	Naomi Stadlen	£9.99
0 7499 2439 X	When Your Kids Push Your Buttons	Bonnie Harris	£10.99

All Piatkus titles are available from:

Piatkus Books Ltd, c/o Bookpost, PO Box 29, Douglas,
Isle of Man, IM99 1BQ

Telephone (+44) 01624 677 237
Fax (+44) 01624 670 923
Email: bookshop@enterprise.net
Free Postage and Packing in the United Kingdom
Credit Cards accepted. All Cheques payable to Bookpost

Prices and availability are subject to change without prior notice. Allow 14 days for delivery. When placing orders, please state if you do not wish to receive any additional information.